Zimbabwe

Zimbabwe

BY BARBARA RADCLIFFE ROGERS
AND STILLMAN D. ROGERS

Enchantment of the World
Second Series

Children's Press®

A Division of Scholastic Inc.

NEW YORK TORONTO LONDON AUCKLAND SYDNEY
MEXICO CITY NEW DELHI HONG KONG
DANBURY, CONNECTICUT

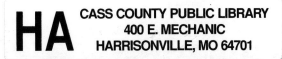

Frontispiece: A village is dwarfed by a huge boabab tree.

Consultant: Dr. Richard Saunders, assistant professor of African politics in the Department of Political Science, York University

Please note: All statistics are as up-to-date as possible at the time of publication.

Book Production by Herman Adler Design

Library of Congress Cataloging-in-Publication Data

Rogers, Barbara Radcliffe.
    Zimbabwe / by Barbara Radcliffe Rogers and Stillman D. Rogers.
        p. cm. — (Enchantment of the world. Second series)
    Includes bibliographical references and index.
    ISBN 0-516-21113-7
    1. Zimbabwe—Juvenile literature. [1. Zimbabwe.] I. Title. II. Series.
DT2889 .R64 2002
968.91—dc21   00-066040

Printed in the United States of America.
1 2 3 4 5 6 7 8 9 10 R 11 10 09 08 07 06 05 04 03 02

Acknowledgments

The authors would like to thank Juliette Rogers and the Brown University Department of Anthropology for their assistance with the research.

Contents

Cover photo:
A Zimbabwe girl
balances a sack
on her head.

The Great Zimbabwe

Tonga children

A Picture
of Africa

Elephants and buffalo at Lake Kariba

Opposite: **Victoria Falls**

Whial do you picture in your mind when you think of Africa? Is it a lion lying under a large tree? Is it a wide landscape of waving yellow grasses with a family of elephants walking across it? Perhaps it is a village of round homes with pointed thatched roofs. Or people gathered together at colorful markets. Chances are that at least one of these pictures will jump into your mind.

A traditional village

A Picture of Africa **9**

Geopolitical map of Zimbabwe

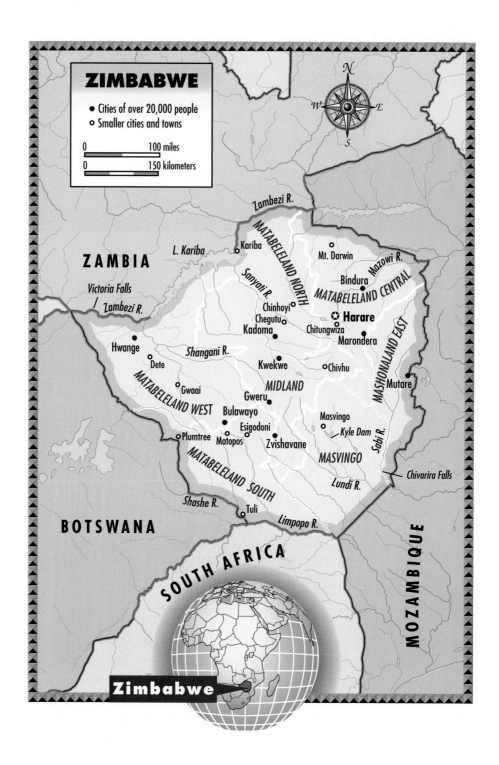

ZIMBABWE

- Cities of over 20,000 people
- Smaller cities and towns

0 — 100 miles
0 — 150 kilometers

Zambezi R.

ZAMBIA

L. Kariba

Kariba

○ Mt. Darwin

MATABELELAND NORTH

Sanyati R.

Mozowi R.

Bindura

MATABELELAND CENTRAL

Chinhoyi

Victoria Falls

Zambezi R.

Chegutu

✪ **Harare**

Kadoma

Chitungwiza

Marondera

MASHONALAND EAST

Hwange

○ Dete

Shangani R.

Kwekwe

○ Chivhu

Mutare

○ Gwaai

MATABELELAND WEST

Gweru

MIDLAND

Bulawayo

Masvingo

○ Esigodoni

~ Kyle Dam

Sabi R.

○ Plumtree

Matopos

Zvishavane

MASVINGO

MATABELELAND SOUTH

Chivarira Falls

Lundi R.

Shashe R.

Tuli

Limpopo R.

BOTSWANA

SOUTH AFRICA

MOZAMBIQUE

Zimbabwe

You could see any of these scenes in Zimbabwe. But exciting wild animals and colorful village life are just the beginning of this African country's interesting sights. Victoria Falls, Africa's largest waterfall and one of the most dramatic in the world, drops suddenly at Zimbabwe's border, sending up a cloud of mist that can be seen for miles.

Africa's largest and most mysterious ruin, called the Great Zimbabwe, was built by the ancestors of today's Zimbabweans. Cave paintings all over the country tell us how Stone Age people lived there. Gracious cities with parks between tall buildings are the busy commercial centers. Take a trip with us through this exciting country to meet its warm people and exotic wildlife, and to find out more about the land where the earliest humans once walked.

A park in Harare, the capital city

The Land Between Two Rivers

THE GEOGRAPHY AND THE GEOLOGY OF THE AREA OF southern Africa known as Zimbabwe have had a tremendous impact on the country's history, economy, and way of life. They brought the British, who occupied the land, and they influenced their choice of settlements. The unique formation of the land—its soils and its mineral wealth—has impacted the economy even into the era of independence. It will certainly continue to shape the country for many generations.

Looking at the Land

The total land area of Zimbabwe is 150,872 square miles (390,728 square kilometers). This relatively small nation is land-locked—bordered by four countries that surround it on all sides. To the north and east, Zimbabwe shares its longest border with Mozambique. Zambia sits to the north and northwest, and Botswana shares a lengthy border along the southwest. Zimbabwe also shares a relatively short border with South Africa's Northern Province (called the Transvaal on some maps) to the south. That border is formed by the Limpopo River.

The Limpopo and the Zambezi Rivers so define the location of Zimbabwe that many people in South Africa simply say "North of the Limpopo" to refer to the country. The Zambezi is a natural boundary that separates southern Africa from central Africa.

Zimbabwe's most prominent geological feature is a broad ridge that spans the country from the northeast to the southwest,

Mount Inyangani, the
highest point in Zimbabwe

A satellite view of the
Great Dyke

known as the highveld. Covering 145,108 square miles (375,801 sq km), this ridge averages a width of 50 miles (80 km). It reaches its highest point at Mount Inyangani, the highest elevation in the country at 8,504 feet (2,592 meters).

The remarkable nature of this land comes from its geologic origins. The region was formed by molten rocks and mineral matter that spewed out from under the surface. Granite more than 3 billion years old defines the surface of the land, which was shaped into erratic formations as molten minerals flowed over the ragged granite and were deposited in crevices. These deposits are called *schists*. The result of this is a mineral-rich landscape that has been prized for its gold deposits since they were first discovered by native peoples. Much of the landscape still consists of large granite formations.

About 650 million years ago, movements in Earth's crust created an area known

Zimbabwe's Geographical Features

Highest Elevation: Mount Inyangani, 8,504 feet (2,592 m)

Lowest Elevation: Near Dumela at the Limpopo River's exit into Mozambique, 660 feet (201 m)

Greatest Distance North to South: 519 miles (835 km)

Greatest Distance East to West: 451 miles (726 km)

Longest River: Sabi River, 400 miles (644 km)

Largest Artificial Lake: Lake Kariba, 175 by 20 miles (282 by 32 km)

Largest Urban Population: Harare, 1,184,000

Hottest Location: Zambezi Valley

Largest Waterfall: Victoria Falls

Longest Bridge: Birchenough Bridge, over the Sabi River

today as the Great Rift Valley. This giant tear in Earth's crust spanned eastern Africa, becoming smaller as it moved south. The Great Dyke is a narrow section of the edge of that tear that extends north–south through the highveld region of Zimbabwe. Today, it stands as a ridge of low hills that run for 320 miles (515 km) and reach heights as much as 1,500 feet (457 m) above sea level. The Great Dyke contains several precious metals and nonprecious metals and minerals, including gold, silver, and platinum, as well as tin, nickel, and asbestos.

The Karoo System is a geological region covering 600,000 square miles (1,553,880 sq km). It is made up of layers of sedimentary rock, in some places as thick as 35,000 feet (10,668 m), which is mostly sandstone, shale, volcanic deposits, and ancient rock that dates as far back as 286 million years.

This region is economically important because of its deposits of coal. It is historically important for the fossil evidence contained in its layers. They help scientists understand the evolution of reptiles into mammals.

Coal lies under sandstone and shale in this part of the Karoo System.

The Veld

The *veld* is the general term used to describe the land of southern Africa, especially land that is farmed and worked. This is the savannas and the bushlands—broad expanses of open land with grasses, and low brush with scattered trees. The veld of Zimbabwe, and also of the surrounding areas in southern Africa, is divided into three major categories that are determined (and named) by general elevation. These are the *highveld*, the *middleveld*, and the *lowveld*. Other sub-categories include regionally used terms such as *bush veld*, *grass veld*, and *thorn veld*, named for their unique vegetation.

The Highveld

The highveld is a strip of elevated land that crosses Zimbabwe at an angle from the southwest to the northeast. Because of its favorable climate, with lower temperatures than the lower river valleys, this is the region the British settled. It reaches an average elevation of 4,000 to 6,000 feet (1,220 to 1,830 m) above sea level. The northeastern region reaches elevations of more than 8,000 feet (2,440 m). Its highest point is near the Mozambique border at the peak of Mount Inyangani, 8,504 feet (2,592 m) above sea level.

The highveld creates the watershed line for Zimbabwe. In other words, it is like a high backbone, and all rivers and their tributaries flow either north–west or south–east from its heights. The land of the highveld is generally flat and even, occasionally topped with stony hills called *kopjes*. The sandy soil of this temperate region is not very good for farming, and it erodes easily.

A granite kopje

Looking at Zimbabwe's Cities

Bulawayo (below) is the largest city in Zimbabwe after Harare. It lies in the savanna in the southwestern part of the country. Once the capital of Ndebele leader Lobengula's kingdom, Bulawayo was occupied by the British in 1893. They founded the modern city nearby in 1894. Today, Bulawayo is a regional industrial and transportation center with a population of 621,000. Landmarks include the Natural History Museum and the Railway Museum. Temperatures average 57°F (14°C) in July and 70°F (21°C) in January.

Chitungwiza is Zimbabwe's third-largest city and its largest township, adjoining Harare. Industries include textile and food production and engineering. It is home to 274,000 people.

Mutare is the fourth-largest city in Zimbabwe. Most of its 132,000 residents are Shona. It lies along the Mozambique border in the foothills of the Eastern Highlands. Mutare is the primary transportation center of the region, serving as land-locked Zimbabwe's link to the Indian Ocean via the Mozambique port of Beira. Local industries include forestry, gold mining, agriculture, and tourism.

The Middleveld

Rising to an average elevation between 2,000 and 4,000 feet (610 and 1,220 m) above sea level, the middleveld of Zimbabwe is situated on the downslope of the highveld. Most of this region is characterized by this declining elevation. Because of its downhill slope, it is plagued by the constant erosion of an already poor layer of topsoil.

The Lowveld

Zimbabwe's granite covering has, over time, left the lowveld with very sandy and infertile topsoil. The soil is coarse, so it does not hold moisture well. The better soil for farming is made of clays and loams, but it is rarer here.

The weather patterns of the lowveld compound many farming problems. The rainy season brings fast-and-furious storms. The rain falls so quickly and in such volume that the soil, which is sandy and poorly equipped to hold the moisture, often just washes away. This erosion can wash away entire farms and carry away large amounts of topsoil. In addition, the soil does not contain enough of the minerals needed to support constant farming. It has generous deposits of minerals for mining, however.

Soil erosion caused by heavy rains

The prehistoric volcanic activity and shifts in Earth's crust left behind fault lines, or cracks. Many of these have become beds for major rivers and provide drainage for rainwater. The Zambezi River flows through a major fault that extends to the west. The Sabi and the Limpopo Rivers also flow through depressions created by fault lines. These three rivers are responsible for draining the entire country.

The Zambezi River, which forms the border between Zimbabwe and Zambia, was dammed in 1959 to create electricity, forming one of the world's largest artificial lakes. Lake Kariba (in the local, Tonka language, *kariba* means "little trap") is 175 miles (282 km) long and at its widest point is 20 miles (32 km) across. The dam wall is 128 feet (39 m) tall

This dam formed Lake Kariba in 1959.

Victoria Falls

One of the largest waterfalls in the world, Victoria Falls spans 5,604 feet (1,708 m), with a height that reaches up to 355 feet (108 m). This is twice the height of Niagara Falls, and one-and-a-half times its width. The falls is most active during April, when 163,680,000 gallons (620,000 kiloliters) of water rush over it each minute. This great force of water falling creates a cloud of spray that can reach up to 1,650 feet (more than 500 m) into the air. The impressive cloud hosts lovely rainbows during most daylight hours as the sun shines through the water drops. At certain times and from certain vantage points, it is also possible to see a "lunar rainbow," as the moon's light passes through the mist of the falls. The spray cloud from the falls covers the surrounding area with enough water to sustain a rain forest.

Victoria Falls is one of the most important tourist attractions of southern Africa, and unlike most water-falls, it is very easy to see. This is because the water falls over the rim of a deep crack in Earth, and the Zambezi River then flows off to the side, along the crack. The opposite wall of this crack faces the falls directly, providing many perfect views of the face of the falls.

The falls were named by Dr. David Livingstone (below), who was the first European to come upon the magnificent sight. His historic journal entry of November 16, 1855, records the awe with which he beheld the falls: "On sights as beautiful as this, angels in their flight must have gazed." He named the falls after the British queen, Victoria. The African name for the falls, *Mosi-o-Tunya*, means "smoke that thunders." This refers to the cloud of spray that hangs over the falls and the roaring of the water, which can be heard from many miles away.

Queen Victoria

Victoria Falls was named for Queen Victoria, who ruled as monarch of Great Britain longer than any other king or queen. Born on May 24, 1819, she was the daughter of Edward, Duke of Kent, the fourth son of King George III. She became queen in 1837 and reigned until her death on January 22, 1901. She was so popular that many places around the world are named for her, including the city of Victoria in British Columbia, Canada, and the state of Victoria in Australia.

and has six floodgates. The Zambezi is subject to frequent floods, so building the dam was a major feat of engineering.

Such dams are very important in Zimbabwe because they are an important source of electricity and of water for irrigation. The dam on Lake Mutirikwi (formerly Lake Kyle), near Masvingo, was built in 1961 to irrigate the sugar and citrus farms around it.

The Sabi River, also called the Save, begins in the highveld of Zimbabwe, in the northern region, just about 50 miles (80 km) south of Harare. The Sabi flows southeast, then dips on a southerly course as it meets with the Odzi River. The Sabi reaches the Mozambique border at the Chivirira Falls, whose name translates as "place of boiling." After the falls, the Sabi makes a distinct turn east and very slightly north and flows into the Indian Ocean near Mambone, Mozambique.

Altogether, the Sabi River flows for 400 miles (644 km). Although it cannot be navigated and used for transportation, the river has been very useful in developing irrigation systems in the lowveld in the eastern region of the country. The river provides water for about 370,000 acres (150,000 hectares) of farmland.

The Limpopo River originates as the Krokodil (Crocodile) River in South Africa. As it winds on its northern path, it forms the border between South Africa's Northern Province and Botswana for about 250 miles (400 km), where its name changes to the Limpopo. As the river turns to flow east, it becomes Zimbabwe's southern border with South Africa.

Where this border meets the Mozambique border, the river turns into a series of rapids that drop 800 feet (244 m). It then begins to shift to a southeasterly course, finally emptying into the Indian Ocean on the southern coast of Mozambique.

The Limpopo, including the Krokodil section, flows for a total of 1,120 miles (1,800 km). This river is not useful for transport for most of its length, except for a distance of about 130 miles (209 km) from its mouth in Mozambique. This section is cut in half by a dam, so use of the river for trade is quite limited. The Limpopo was once named the Espiritu Santo River, by Vasco da Gama, the first European explorer to see it.

Climate

The easiest way to really see where the climate is most comfortable in Zimbabwe is to look at a map. All the major cities and roads lie across the country at an angle, outlining the highveld. These higher elevations and milder temperatures influenced both the native peoples and, more noticeably, the colonial occupation. The white settlers found these areas much more comfortable, and they settled them in preference

Mutare is in the comfortable climate of the highveld.

to the lower, hotter regions. This led to the rise of cities, urban areas, and general population in the highveld.

In general, Zimbabwe has a subtropical climate, with weather between that of the tropics and temperate zones. Temperatures in Harare, which is in the northern section of the highveld at an altitude of 4,833 feet (1,473 m), average 78 degrees Fahrenheit (26 degrees Celsius) at their highest in January. June temperatures are milder, reaching a high of 70°F (21°C). The average yearly rainfall for the city is 33 inches (83 centimeters), with a high of 7.7 inches (19.6 cm) in January. There is seldom any rain at all in June.

The climate of regions at an elevation of more than 4,000 feet (or 1,200 m) is considered to be warm-temperate. At higher elevations, especially from 4,000 to 5,000 feet (or 1,200 to 1,500 m), frost is common at night during the much cooler, drier season from April to August. From November to February, the temperatures in this higher region are warmer because of the more powerful rays of the sun, and the humidity level is higher, too. Humidity—the moisture content of the air—magnifies the degree to which humans feel the heat, making us more uncomfortable. This is the most uncomfortable time of year. The seasons here are the reverse of those in North America because Zimbabwe lies south of the equator.

At lower elevations, the temperatures rise. The lowlands experience the hottest temperatures, especially between October and February. This climate is considered tropical. As in the higher elevations, the most humid season—called the rainy season—is during this time.

Rain in Zimbabwe almost always comes in sudden, torrential downpours. Often these are thunderstorms that come and go relatively quickly, dumping all their rain in a short time. This type of storm makes erosion even worse because of the force with which the water comes down. It is also a problem because the land does not have as much time to soak up the water. It runs off too quickly because so much falls at once. As the temperature rises and the elevation decreases, the average rainfall decreases, leaving the hotter regions drier, too.

A rainstorm in Harare

Where the Lion Is King

An eastern forest in springtime

Opposite: **Zebras near a wooded area**

SAVANNAS AND WOODLANDS COVER MOST OF ZIMBABWE. The savannas are open grasslands with wooded areas. True forests grow in the eastern border region and north of Bulawayo. Rain is fairly abundant in the summer, encouraging many varieties of plants to grow and covering Zimbabwe with colorful flowers and blooming trees.

The savannas and their open forests make a perfect habitat for many of the wild animals we picture first when we think of Africa—elephants, lions, leopards, giraffes, cheetahs, baboons, and zebras. In fact, Hwange National Park, in western Zimbabwe, is one of the best places in Africa to see wild animals. It has the highest concentrations of elephants and many other animals.

A Varied Landscape

Even though Zimbabwe is mostly covered in grasslands and trees, its scenery is far from boring. Each region has its own kinds of plants, based on its altitude, its rainfall, and even its history.

Where the great central plateau slopes down to the valley of the Zambezi River, the forests are thick with many varieties of trees. Teak and mahogany, both highly prized furniture and building woods, are plentiful. Ebony, a wood valued for its stonelike hardness, grows here as well. Mopane, musasa, and acacia are other common trees. In fact, Zimbabwe has a much greater variety of tree species than many parts of Europe or the Americas.

This forest is a favorite habitat of elephants and giraffes, which feed on the tender shoots of the treetops. Buffalos, cheetahs, lions, sables, zebras, wildebeests, impalas, leopards, elands, waterbucks, and gemsboks all find homes here.

Along the banks of the Zambezi River and gigantic Lake Kariba—formed when the river was dammed in 1959—grow different trees and plants. These thrive in the moist environment, surviving changes in water level that can leave them high and dry or under several feet of water. Here the most common trees are the mopane, the baobab, and the thorn tree, a type of acacia. None of these is an important commercial wood, but each has a distinctive shape that gives the landscape its character. Baobabs are huge trees with very fat trunks. They usually stand alone in the low grasslands.

The highveld and the middleveld are covered in tall grass and plants, which catch and spread wildfires easily. The roots survive the fires to send up new grasses the following season. Trees are not usually so resistant to fire, so the major trees in this area are varieties of *Brachystegia*, which can survive the frequent burn-over of the grass veld.

Wildfires control growth in the savanna woodlands.

Unlike the lowveld of Zimbabwe's neighbor, South Africa, where farming has changed the plants, Zimbabwe's lowveld still has most of its natural grasses. Most of Zimbabwe's corn and all of its tobacco, two major crops, are grown on the highveld, with some corn also grown on the middleveld.

Wildlife Habitat

An area of 5,600 square miles (14,500 sq km) is protected in Hwange National Park, one of the largest nature reserves in Africa. It is about the size of the state of Connecticut. Inside the park is some of the best game viewing on the continent, with the most species— more than 100 kinds of mammal and 400 varieties of bird.

Thirsty animals drinking from a pan in Hwange National Park

In the dry season (August through October), these animals move closer to water sources in the pans or low hollows where water gathers. Animals drink the water, wallow in the mud, and eat the salt that accumulates as the waters evaporate in the hot sun. These watering places are among Africa's best locations to see wild animals. A single Hwange buffalo herd may have 1,000 animals in it.

More than 14,000 elephants gather here in the winter. One reason for the large number is that elephants at Hwange have smaller tusks than those in other parts of Africa, probably because their diet is low in minerals. Having a poor diet

Elephants gathered along a river

is actually good for their health, because smaller tusks protect them from being killed for their ivory by poachers. Many elephants gather in Hwange because the forests cannot support them, and game managers must cull the herds regularly.

Along with buffalo and elephant, the park is a good place to see lions, and even hard-to-spot leopards and cheetahs. Zebras and giraffes are common, as are wildebeests, and all the grazing animals, such as impalas, elands, sables, and gemsboks. In its rivers are hippopotamuses and crocodiles, as well as many waterbirds. The wide variety of wild animals and birds makes Hwange a popular center for safaris and big-game hunting. Local programs such as CAMPFIRE (Community Management Programme for Indigenous Resources) involve local communities in these tourist activities, a boost for the local economy.

Mana Pools National Park surrounds a series of small lakes formed by old channels of the Zambezi River. Fed by floodwaters in times of heavy rain, the pools are home to many fish and to waterbirds, which nest along its shores. Wild animals

National Parks and Reserves

(F) Forest Reserve (M) National Monument (NP) National Park
(R) Recreatonal Park (S) Sanctuary (W) Wilderness

1	Chimanimani (NP)	12	Matusadona (NP)
2	Chinhoyi Caves (NP)	13	Mavuradonha (W)
3	Chirinda (F)	14	Mutirikwe (R)
4	Chizarira (NP)	15	Mtarazi Falls (NP)
5	Hwange (NP)	16	Mushandike (S)
6	Gona-re-Zhou (NP)	17	Ngezi (R)
7	Great Zimbabwe (M)	18	Nyanga (NP)
8	Kazuma Pan (NP)	19	Sebakwe (R)
9	Lake Chivero (R)	20	Vumba (F)
10	Mana Pools (NP)	21	Zambezi/
11	Matobo (NP)		Victoria Falls (NP)

A hippo bathing at Mana Pools National Park

A Historic National Symbol

The eagle shown on Zimbabwe's flag represents the carved stone bird found at the Great Zimbabwe and other archeological sites. No one really knows their symbolic significance. Both the martial eagle (below) and the bataleur eagle live in Zimbabwe today.

are abundant in the 848-square-mile (2,196-sq-km) park around the lakes, especially hippos, elephants, buffalos, rhinoceroses, lions, leopards, crocodiles, and antelopes.

While lions and crocodiles might seem like dangerous neighbors, there are few cases of people being hurt by these animals. Zimbabweans know not to swim in rivers where crocodiles are common, and even children have a healthy respect for wild animals.

More dangerous are some much smaller creatures. The mosquito, for instance, carries malaria. This disease is especially dangerous to children, who dehydrate (lose the liquids in their body) from the high fevers it brings. And more common in the rivers than crocodiles is the bilharzia worm, a very tiny parasite that lives in freshwater all over Africa. People who drink from or swim in these waters pick up the worm, which lays its eggs inside their veins and makes them sick.

Rare Animals

In southern Zimbabwe, on the Mozambique border, Gona-re-Zhou Game Park covers 1,930 square miles (5,000 sq km) where elephant and a rare variety of nyala antelope are protected. The park is well named: *Gona-re-Zhou* means "elephant refuge." The area was made into a park in 1967 after a giant elephant was shot here. This elephant was well known to the local people as *Dhlulamithi*, which means "taller than the treetops." Its tusks weighed 106 and 137 pounds (48 and 62 kilograms), the largest ever recorded in southern Africa.

Also found here is the king, or striped, cheetah, which is somewhat larger than the common cheetah and has unusual striped markings instead of the usual spots. Fewer than two dozen of these animals exist anywhere in the world. Crocodiles and hippos are common in the Lundi River, which crosses the reserve.

Predators

In the food chain, many animals live by using smaller or slower animals as food. They are called *predators*. There is nothing bad about the animals that eat meat; this is simply their nature. They play their part in keeping wildlife in

A cheetah chasing a gazelle

balance by controlling populations of other species. Some of Zimbabwe's predators are the lion, the leopard, the cheetah, the serval, the civet, the hyena, the jackal, and the bat-eared fox.

Is the Lion Really Lazy?

Many people say that the male lion is lazy because he lets the female catch his food, then eats his fill before she and the cubs are allowed to eat. But we cannot impose human behavior on wild creatures, and lions' habits are given to them by nature for a good reason. The female lion is smaller and faster than the more powerful, heavier male. She is much more skillful at hunting and can spring great distances and run very fast. But she is not as powerful a fighter as the male. His job is to protect her and, especially, the small cubs from other animals so they can grow up to be adults and carry on the species. Each member of a lion family does the job it can do best.

Places for Plants

Large animals are not the only wildlife that are given a special home in Zimbabwe. About 2 miles (3.2 km) north of Harare is the National Botanic Garden. Its more than 5,000 trees include examples of 750 species that grow in Zimbabwe. Harare Gardens, in the city center, covers 37 acres (15 hectares) and features a miniature replica of Victoria Falls that even has a rainbow.

Ewanrigg Botanical Gardens, on the eastern edge of Harare, was once the farm of a plant collector named Basil Christian. He left the property to the nation as a park when he died. Its collection of aloes—tall plants with dramatic red flowers and thick spiked leaves—is the largest in southern Africa. These plants bloom and are most colorful in the winter.

The flame lily is Zimbabwe's national flower.

Chimanimani National Park covers a short mountain range only 28 miles (45 km) long, but very beautiful. Its plant life is nourished by the minerals in the rich, stony soil, with dozens of wildflower species and forests of cedar and yellowwood trees. Mixed with these are tropical ferns and orchids.

One of the great floral showplaces of Zimbabwe is Vumba National Park, whose gardens are known for azaleas, begonias, proteas, lilies, and gladioli, as well as for ferns. Nearby is the Bunga Forest, where 250 varieties of fern grow in its misty woods. Locals called this area *mubvumbi*, which means "mountains of drizzle."

Blooming flamboyant trees arch over a city street.

Colorful Trees

Harare is known for its parks and gardens, as well as for its colorful blooming trees. Entire streets are shaded by the spreading limbs of brilliant red poinciana, also called flamboyant trees. Others are lined with jacaranda, which turns whole neighborhoods purple with its blossoms in the spring.

Musasa trees change color in the spring, which is September and October in Zimbabwe, much as the maples and other hardwoods of North America do in the same months. As the musasa's new leaves appear and grow, they change from bright red to plum color, finally becoming green. The attractive small town of Shurugwe is known for its streets of musasa trees.

Plants From Far Away

Although southern Africa is home to more plant species than any other place in the world, not all the plants there are natives. European traders and colonists brought many new plants, both for ornament and for their economic value. Tea was one of these, planted first in South Africa in the 1850s and now grown in eastern Zimbabwe, in the highland plantations of the Pungwe Valley. Tea is a very popular drink in Zimbabwe.

Timber Trees

Many trees that grow naturally in Zimbabwe's forests are valuable for commercial uses.

Zimbabwe teak: Teak trees grow to 60 feet (18 m) tall with trunks 3 feet (1 m) in diameter. Teak is used for beautiful floors, strong railway ties, and furniture. The Ndebele call it *mgusi* and use it to make dugout canoes.

Bloodwood: Slightly taller and bigger around than the teak tree, bloodwood is a strong, long-lasting wood used for furniture. The Karanga call it *mukwa* and once made paddles, canoes, and spear shafts from it. The bark, roots, flowers, and leaves are used as medicines.

Mahogany: Red mahogany is known to grow as tall as 590 feet (180 m) with a trunk 16.5 feet (5 m) in diameter. White mahogany is smaller, only about 66 feet (20 m) tall and with a trunk width of 5 feet (1.5 m). The wood of white mahogany is soft and easy to carve, making it a favorite of artists who use it for masks, statues, and wooden implements such as ladles. Oil from mahogany seeds is used to make soap.

White farmers planted another *exotic*, which is the name for plants that do not grow naturally, but have been brought from another place. They planted rows of eucalyptus trees as windbreaks and to use for fuel. These grow quickly, but they also reproduce quickly and have spread to cover entire areas. Tobacco and corn, two main crops in Zimbabwe, were also introduced from other places.

Environmental Issues

Poaching rhinoceros for its horn, an illegal practice, has killed most of the country's herd of black rhino, once the largest in the world. Other environmental problems face Zimbabwe, too. Deforestation, soil erosion, and the pollution of the rivers all concern naturalists and others who value Zimbabwe's unique ecosystem.

A ranger examining poached rhinoceros horns

People in Motion

W HILE IT IS WELL ACCEPTED THAT HUMANS FIRST WALKED the Earth in Africa, the earliest history of people is shrouded in mystery. For many thousands of years, humans have wandered the African continent settling new areas, warring on others for the best lands, and moving on to different lands to avoid war.

These African peoples did not keep a written history of their movements. Archeologists—who study ancient cultures by looking at their physical remains—and anthropologists—who study customs, languages, and beliefs—now think that most people who live in Zimbabwe are descended from people who came from the part of Africa now called Cameroon. They were from a group who spoke one of the Bantu family of languages.

In Zimbabwe, they became known as the *Shona*, a name that originally referred to the ruler of the tribe. The word later came to mean all of the people within that language group. They settled in the highland plateau in what we now call Zimbabwe, and along the coast of the neighboring Mozambique.

Opposite: **Prehistoric cave painting in Zimbabwe**

Language Families

The term *family of languages* is used to describe a group of languages that have differences but that developed from one language. In Europe, for example, French, Spanish, and Italian are different, but they share certain features, and they all developed from Latin. The Shona language developed from ancient West African language. It is related to several other African languages.

Archeologists have not been able to tell exactly when Shona-speaking people first came to Zimbabwe. Some evidence shows that they may have come as early as the year A.D. 200. Evidence found in different pottery styles points to a date around the year A.D. 900, but most indicates that the earlier date is the more probable. Solving this mystery is one of the great tasks for modern archeologists.

Pottery fragments help scientists learn about the first peoples in Zimbabwe.

In about 500 B.C., when the people of the biblical era were actively building their cultures and ruling northern Africa, the area we call Zimbabwe had very few people. Most of them were from the Khosa family of peoples. They did not settle in one spot, but hunted and gathered wild foods using stone tools. A little more than 300 years later, the first signs of pottery began to appear. By A.D. 200 they began farming, herding animals, building houses, and using iron. This early settlement culture is called the Chifumbaze period, the early Iron Age.

Studies of pottery fragments found by archeologists show that over the next 700 years people became more sophisticated.

By the year 900, people in tribal areas began to organize a basic government. They shifted from a subsistence style of life, in which they lived on what they could find and make themselves, to one in which they traded goods with other people. By the year 1000, the Muslims of North Africa made contact with the early Shona people and began to trade goods for gold. Shortly after the first millennium, in about 1075, the first real communities began to develop. A village called Gumanye was built on a hilltop at an area now called the Great Zimbabwe.

The Great Zimbabwe

The word *zimbabwe* refers to an important village, a "capital," which is the headquarters of an important person such as a chief. The Great Zimbabwe is thought to be the earliest and

Ruins of the Great Zimbabwe

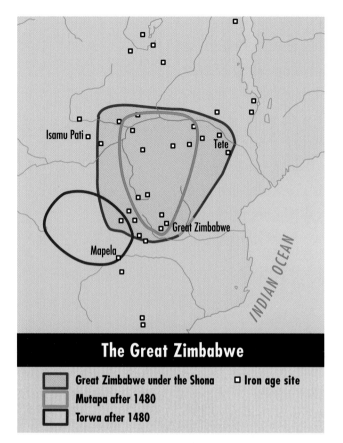

The Great Zimbabwe

- Great Zimbabwe under the Shona
- Mutapa after 1480
- Torwa after 1480
- □ Iron age site

the greatest of these major African urban settlements. At some point just before the year 1300, the people at Gumanye began enhancing their village by building stone walls. Over the next century or so and until about 1400, these walls became extensive, covering a large area. Early archeologists thought that the walls supported tall roofs of huge buildings, but more recent studies show that the walls were actually built to provide privacy and as security for the wood, mud, and thatch buildings that were built within the enclosures.

Builders of the Great Zimbabwe found that by building fires on open ledges of local granite, they could break the rock into flat stones that they could stack to form walls. They also discovered gold in the stones of the hills around them. The trade in gold and other goods made many people wealthy. As wealth spread, smaller but still important zimbabwes were built over the large, crescent-shaped plateau.

The people who built the Great Zimbabwe were the leaders of what was probably the first great state in Zimbabwe. Why the Great Zimbabwe declined and was abandoned is unknown, but we do know that by the end of the 1500s, its wealth and power had ended.

Torwa and Mutapa

At the same time, two more states arose, one on the southern end of the plateau and another on the northern end. Late in the 1600s, Portuguese traders sailed around the Cape of Good Hope and the southern tip of Africa to the coast of Mozambique. The first Europeans to reach the area, they quickly replaced the Muslims as the major traders. The records of these Portuguese traders tell us what we know about the leaders of these two states.

In the southwest, a state called Torwa grew. Its capital was at Kame, where it remained for 200 years until it was destroyed by fire. In the north, the center of building was the Mutapa state. The Torwa people used and adapted the building techniques of the Great Zimbabwe, but the people of Mutapa abandoned such stone construction early, and less is known about their history.

In the 1640s, a war broke out between two factions that wanted control of Torwa, and it is probably at this time that Kame was burned. One of the leaders invited the Portuguese to join the war on his side and they won, setting up a new capital at Danangombe. It was smaller than Kame but more elaborate. This state did not last very long, however, ending about 1683.

Life at the Top

While the people of the Great Zimbabwe built tall stone walls around their houses, those of Torwa used the same principles to build a series of stepped stone terraces around hills. The houses of the rulers were then built at the top.

Visiting the Kame ruins

Fragments of Chinese pottery found at a Portuguese trading site

At the same time that Torwa was developing in the south, Mutapa was developing in the north. Legend says that a leader named Mutota left the Great Zimbabwe between 1425 and 1450 and established a new state called Mutapa, named for the title of its leader. Mutapa controlled a large area by 1490.

By the end of the next century, it controlled lands from the Zimbabwe plateau all the way to the coast. The people of Mutapa traded heavily with the Portuguese, and the Portuguese recorded much of their history after 1490.

The Portuguese Influence

The Portuguese set up their own armies to protect their trading outposts. These armies were called *sertanejos*, and in time they included many black locals in their ranks. These armies were one of the ways in which Portuguese traders differed from the Muslims. Another was that by 1560 the Portuguese had decided to take over Mutapa and its gold mines for themselves. Their first attempt, under the leadership of Francisco Barreto, was made in 1571–1576. It ended in failure.

Over the next 125 years, the Portuguese continued their attacks on Mutapa, seizing land and gold mines. Mutapa remained a state, and it wasn't until the 1690s that the Portuguese were ousted. Leadership disputes continued to disrupt the state until war ended it in the 1830s.

The Changamire

While the Portuguese were expanding their influence over the Mutapa and the Torwa were fighting each other in the mid-1600s, a new state was forming and growing. This new power was led by the Changamire and his people, the Rozvi. Starting in the southwest in the 1670s, the Changamire and the Rozvi took over Torwa without a serious battle and made Danangombe their own capital.

In the early 1690s, the Changamire-Rozvi extended their reach, driving the Portuguese from the Zimbabwe plateau and inland areas. The Changamire state was the strongest and most politically powerful yet, taxing and demanding tribute from weaker states.

With the Changamire expulsion of the Portuguese, the Mutapa state recovered some of its former authority. From the 1690s until the 1830s, both Mutapa and Changamire remained independent, with Changamire having the strongest army south of the Zambezi until the 1830s. Both states recognized that they needed the goods they could get from the Portuguese, and both continued to trade with them.

People on the Move

Early in the 1800s, a series of wars in South Africa caused large-scale movements of people away from areas that had been their traditional homelands. This included a large number of Nguni-speaking people, some of whom went north across the Limpopo River and into the lands of Zimbabwe and Mozambique. Known as fierce fighters, they began a period of expansion known as the *mfecane*, or "time of great troubles." In the 1830s, these Nguni speakers, called Ngoni, moved into the southern part of the Zimbabwe plateau. Pushing into the Changamire territory, they destroyed the capital at Danangombe and killed the Changamire. They moved on quickly leaving a weak and leaderless state behind them.

On the heels of the Ngoni came the great leader of the Ndebele, Mzilikazi, who probably was a former ally of the great Zulu leader Shaka. Finding himself an enemy of Shaka, Mzilikazi fled north, raiding the Transvaal of South Africa. Joined by the conquered people, especially the Sotho, Mzilikazi and his followers swarmed into the territory of the weakened Changamire state occupied by the Shona.

Mzilikazi

The founder of one of the great kingdoms of Zimbabwe, Mzilikazi was born about 1790. He was the son of a king and became king of a small tribe called the Kumalo in present-day South Africa. He joined with Shaka, leader of the Zulu, in a war against the British in the 1820s. Shaka turned against him, and Mzilikazi led his tribe through the Transvaal and Botswana, reaching what is now Zimbabwe in 1837. A statesman, he was able to draw the people that he conquered into a new kingdom, known as the Ndebele or Matabele. He organized his people into military townships that fended off Boer intruders in the late 1840s. When Mzilikazi died about 1868, he was entombed in a cave in Ntumbane (right), in the Matopos Hills, which has been guarded ever since by an armed warrior.

The Ndebele became dominant, and even people who spoke Shona adopted the language of this culture. The conquered state accepted Mzilikazi as its new leader. Ndebele became the second most important language group in the Zimbabwe territory. In addition to the peoples of the Shona and the Ndebele language groups, there were two more large groups of people—the Gaza and the Tsonga.

Bulawayo in the late nineteenth century

Sandwiched between the Shona to the north and the Ndebele and Gaza to the south, the Tsonga and the independent Shona groups in the middle were raided by or forced to pay tribute to both sides. The Ndebele were good at attracting their opponents to join them, and by 1890 two-thirds of people calling themselves Ndebele were really of Shona ancestry.

By 1890, all of the major Zimbabwe sites were abandoned, and the life of the people centered in about 9,000 local villages. The only remaining urban site was the Ndebele settlement at Bulawayo, under the leadership of Lobengula.

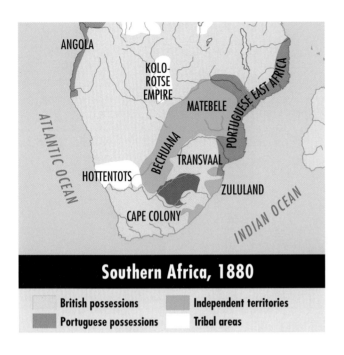

Southern Africa, 1880

British possessions
Portuguese possessions
Independent territories
Tribal areas

ANGOLA
KOLO-ROTSE EMPIRE
MATEBELE
PORTUGUESE EAST AFRICA
BECHUANA
TRANSVAAL
HOTTENTOTS
ZULULAND
CAPE COLONY
ATLANTIC OCEAN
INDIAN OCEAN

European Colonization

Beginning in the 1870s, pressure for colonization began to mount—from the Portuguese in Mozambique to the east, and from the British in South Africa to the south. The Portuguese, lead by Paiva de Andrada, tried to take over the area, but by 1890 they had failed.

It was the British, urged on by their driving leader, Cecil Rhodes, who won the prize. It was Rhodes's

Cecil Rhodes

Cecil John Rhodes (1853–1902) was the dominant figure of southern Africa in the late nineteenth century. Born in England, he went to southern Africa as a young man and, after farming unsuccessfully for two years, began to gain control of diamond mining. He formed a company called DeBeers and became a multimillionaire. In 1881, he was elected to the Cape Colony Parliament. In 1886, he negotiated for British settlers to farm in the lands of the Ndebele. Two years later, he gained control of all mining there. He reached a peace treaty with Lobengula's son, Somabulane, in 1896 at a hill called View of the World in the Matopo Hills near Bulawayo. In accordance with his wish, he was buried on top of View of the World.

Lobengula

When the Ndebele leader Mzilikazi died after a period of civil war, he was succeeded by his son Lobengula, who was born about 1836. Late in his reign, in order to preserve his throne, Lobengula attempted to ally himself with the British from South Africa. First, in 1886, he gave them rights to farm in his lands, and, in 1888, he granted Cecil Rhodes a concession to mine throughout the Ndebele lands.

In 1893, Lobengula sent a group of his men into neighboring lands to recover cattle that had strayed across the border. This brought him into conflict with British settlers sent in by Rhodes.

Within three years, Lobengula's kingdom was gone. He had the royal compound at his capital Bulawayo burned as the British approached, and then he disappeared. He was never heard of again and is thought to have died about 1894.

dream to build a railroad from Cape Colony in South Africa to Cairo, Egypt. To do this he—or Great Britain—had to control the territory in between. He established the British South Africa Company (BSAC) and encouraged settlers to move into the lands of the Ndebele and the Shona. Groups of settlers following BSAC and Rhodes's vision moved into the area, intending eventually to take over the country. Following Shona raids on Ndebele cattle and settlements in 1893, these followers of Rhodes, called Rhodesians, seized the moment. In 1894, they invaded and established a small state.

The Shona and the Ndebele had found the settlers useful as buyers of cattle and as providers of trade goods, but they were overwhelmed as the settlers became powerful. The Rhodesians took the Ndebele's cattle and their best lands, along with the old Changamire gold mines. The natives found themselves working for small wages. Even the Ndebele capital of Bulawayo was taken over by the settlers after the death of Lobengula.

The Rhodesians and the BSAC also settled in the Shona state north of the Ndebele area, and they gradually increased their power as more settlers arrived. There, too, they seized cattle, and they organized native police forces to seize the mines. While the structure of the native state remained in both areas, it was weak and powerless.

Rebellion and Defeat

In 1896, the Ndebele and the Shona again rose in rebellion in a last attempt to reestablish their states and independence, as they existed before 1893. While thousands on all sides engaged in massive killings, each of the native groups fought for the limited goal of reestablishing its own state. Sometimes that meant fighting the other native group as well. Some Ndebele worked with the Rhodesians against the Shona, and some Shona worked with the Rhodesians against the Ndebele. None of the native groups thought of the war in terms of defeating the whole Rhodesian organization. Their defeat in 1897 lay partly in this disunion.

Black workers and their white employer

Following the wars of the 1890s, many things changed for the local peoples. Their local leaders and tribal leadership system remained, but a new system of government was imposed. The people were still allowed to farm on a local trade and barter basis, but the best lands were divided up among white Rhodesian farmers. They brought in local black workers at low wages. The lands were divided up into large tracts, larger than some of the white Rhodesian farmers could manage. The best of the land went to the new Rhodesian farms, and the people who had farmed the land for generations were not allowed to farm them any more.

In other areas, the Shona, the Ndebele, and other, smaller tribal groups were not allowed to train or to take jobs as artisans or supervisors. In business and commerce, they could not take jobs above the level of clerk.

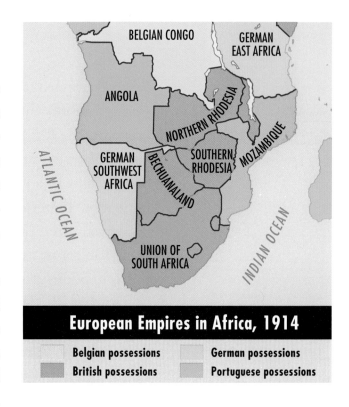

European Empires in Africa, 1914

Belgian possessions   German possessions
British possessions   Portuguese possessions

While primary education—of a sort—was provided, high school education was not made available to black citizens of Rhodesia until 1939. The tribal governments were helpless, only allowed to solve purely local problems among their own people.

Land Seizures

During the 1940s and 1950s, more people were forced off their farms to create bigger farms for the white Rhodesian settlers. The Rhodesian government supported the growth of these big farms with large land grants and money to make sure the farms were profitable. The same government that supported large farms discouraged small peasant farms operated by native peoples.

This continued taking of lands was spurred on by the immigration of more white settlers. Within twenty years of the takeover by the Rhodesians, World War I (1914–1918) ended. Large numbers of war veterans decided to seek their fortunes in Africa because of a lack of jobs and opportunities in England. A little more than twenty-five years later, another wave of settlers arrived after World War II (1939–1945), for the same reasons. On top of these waves of white immigration, Africans came from South Africa seeking jobs in the mines and on the large farms of Rhodesia. Others came from Asia, mostly from India. Rhodesia's population began to soar with all of the new people and from a sudden growth in the native populations.

The colonial situation of Zimbabwe was similar to—yet very different from—that of neighboring South Africa. Native people resented the treatment they received from the new Rhodesian masters. But even though the seizure of land and cattle and limitations on opportunity made blacks angry, governmental repression did not reach the extreme level of the apartheid policies of South Africa.

Pressure for Independence

During the 1950s and 1960s, pressure grew from both the discontented native population and some white Rhodesians. In 1953, in an attempt to strengthen the state, Rhodesia formed a federation with another British colony to the north, called Northern Rhodesia. The union, however, was shortlived and ended in 1964. After its own war of independence, Northern Rhodesia became the country of Zambia.

The Rhodesians were feeling the rising demands of native populations both within Rhodesia and in neighboring countries. In 1964, a native nationalist group killed a white Rhodesian, and the British government decided not to use force to put down the uprising. This decision frightened the white Rhodesian people and led Ian Smith to make a Unilateral Declaration of Independence (UDI) in 1965. Although Great Britain did not recognize the UDI and still considered Rhodesia British territory, for the next fourteen years Rhodesia was an independent country run by a small white minority.

The United Nations (UN) condemned the UDI and urged Britain to take action to stop the rebellion. Many UN member

Ian Douglas Smith

The first native-born Rhodesian to become prime minister of the Rhodesia colony, Ian Smith served in the British Air Corps during World War II, when he was twice shot down. Elected to the Southern Rhodesia Assembly in 1948, he was a member of the Federalist Party. But when the party supported greater representation for black Zimbabweans in 1961, Smith formed the Rhodesian Front, a white supremacist party. In 1962, his new party unexpectedly won the election. In 1964, he was named prime minister. In 1965, he kept his promise to make Rhodesia an independent white state, declaring its independence. After fourteen years, black nationalists forced a 1979 agreement for the independence of Zimbabwe with a predominantly black government, and Smith served briefly in the new government in 1980. He still lives in Harare.

countries, including the United States, followed the organization's call for its members to stop trading with Rhodesia. But even without oil and petroleum products, the UDI lived on.

Rise of Black Nationalism

By the 1950s, Rhodesia had a number of racially different groups. Those in control were the white Rhodesians, most of whom were descended from people who had settled in the area in the 1880s and 1890s. Two other major groups were the Shona and the peoples of the Ndebele state of Mzilikazi. There was also a sizable group of people called *colored* who were descended from unions of black women with white Rhodesian and Asian men.

Native black nationalist feelings rose, and by the 1960s there was an active nationalist movement. In 1957, the nationalists set up their first political party, the African

The black nationalist movement grew strong in the 1960s.

Joshua Nkomo

Probably the best-known Ndebele figure of the twentieth century is Joshua Nkoma. Born in 1917 and educated at the University of Johannesburg in South Africa, he began work with Rhodesian Railways and became active in the labor union. He was named president of the newly formed African National Congress in 1957; escaped to England when it was declared illegal; and returned to Rhodesia in 1960, forming the National Democratic Party and, later, the Zimbabwe African People's Union. The white government of Zimbabwe imprisoned him from 1964 until 1974, when he went to Zambia and organized an army.

Nkomo sought to achieve his goals by negotiation rather than by force. Eventually, his army joined loosely with Robert Mugabe's ZANU from 1976 until independence. In the elections of 1980, he lost to Mugabe. Nkomo was made a member of Mugabe's cabinet

but resigned in 1982, leading to ethnic battles between Ndebele and Shona peoples. In 1987, Nkomo and Mugabe merged their parties in an effort to create unity, and in 1990, Nkomo became a vice president.

National Congress. It was led by Joshua Nkomo, a moderate who sought a peaceful means to political power for Africans.

During 1963, this movement split into two parts—the Zimbabwe African People's Union (ZAPU), and the Zimbabwe African National Union (ZANU). The leader of ZAPU was Joshua Nkomo, and a brash young leader named Robert Mugabe headed ZANU. Mugabe was a radical socialist and follower of the principles of Chairman Mao Tse-tung of China.

For the rest of the 1960s and the 1970s, the two parties worked together and against each other in an uneasy alliance. ZANU put together its army in newly independent Mozambique, which lies along the eastern side of Zimbabwe.

Police patrolling for guerrillas in the early 1970s

Joshua Nkomo assembled his forces in Zambia, to the north. After occasional clashes, the ZANU forces began a war in Rhodesia in 1972. It spread quickly. ZANU sent small units throughout much of the central part of the country and engaged in guerrilla warfare. They attacked white targets at will, everywhere and without warning. ZAPU, more cautious, sent its forces in from Zambia across the western part of the country and dominated in the southwestern areas that were the stronghold of the Ndebele.

The war raged on, and acts of brutality were committed by both sides. Bystanders and people who just got in the way were brutally murdered, but neither side got the upper hand. By the late 1970s, more than 30,000 people had been killed in the war, and all sides had come to the conclusion that they could not win in a reasonable time.

African Tribal Traditions

In many African wars, there has been a strong tribal element. In Rwanda and in Burundi, for example, wars of independence have had strong tribal underpinnings, with rivalries between Hutu and Tutsi being as important as overcoming of the colonial government. In Zimbabwe, however, in spite of the fact that ZANU was headed by a Shona—Robert Mugabe—and ZAPU was headed by a Ndebele—Joshua Nkomo—the conflict remained largely a fight for independence and not a struggle for power between two tribes.

Independence

The standstill caused Great Britain to call for a conference aimed at ending the war. In 1979, meetings were held in London, England, and compromises on both sides led to the independence of Zimbabwe. Blacks had at last assumed control.

Zimbabwe Under Mugabe

In the first elections, held in 1980, ZANU leader Robert Mugabe was elected prime minister of the new republic. His election brought fear to the white Rhodesians, who remembered his earlier Maoist speeches and policies. To many people's surprise, his remarks in his first public statement after his election stressed the need of all peoples to come together for the good of the new state. While he had favored redistribution of the land, after the war, only modest land redistribution

Rhodesian prime minister Abel Muzorewa outside one of the 1979 meetings that led to independence

Joshua Nkomo campaigning before Zimbabwe's first election

Robert Mugabe has led the country since independence.

was made. In spite of a small ZAPU contingent that continued to fight against the new government in the southwest, Mugabe's government took hold, with support from both blacks and whites.

Robert Mugabe has always been the chief executive of Zimbabwe, ever since independence. Even though Mugabe was elected in a multiparty contest, over the years his presidency began to take on features of one-party rule.

Opposition to his rule has come from two separate sources. Some people have begun to challenge what they see as an increasingly corrupt and inbred system controlled at the whim of one man. Others, especially veterans of the wars of independence, have challenged him for failure to deliver on his wartime promise to break up the white farms and give the land to the veterans.

As a result of pressures brought on during elections in 2000, President Mugabe encouraged, or at least approved of, seizures of several large, white-owned farms by people who were primarily veterans of the war for independence. He has also taken the position that since these lands were once taken from the Shona and the Ndebele, the white farmers are not entitled to payment for the land or farms. Mugabe made statements indicating that he would seize the large white farms and redistribute the land. Many farms were taken over by force, and both white and black people—owners, farm workers, and some of the people trying to seize the land—were killed.

President Mugabe seemed to have returned to his wartime promises of land redistribution in order to retain his power in the face of new challenges. These came from a rising new political party, the Movement for Democratic Change (MDC).

Although he was happy to leave the white farmers in peace because their farms produce much of the nation's wealth and food, when his power was threatened, the farmers made easy scapegoats. Even though Zimbabwe's courts have ordered the police to protect the lives and property of the farmers, Mugabe has ordered them to do nothing as the farms are occupied and sometimes destroyed.

Many of the veterans who occupied the farms do not have an agricultural background. They do not have the training, money, equipment, or governmental support to keep these farms produc-

War veterans burning a field of crops

ing. Nor did they plan to. In many cases, they burned crops that were already harvested and ready for sale, along with burning the homes and farm buildings and killing the animals. This left black farm workers who made their living there without jobs. The angry mobs even beat and killed some black workers on these farms. In the spring of 2000, more than 1,000 farms were taken over and their owners and workers driven from their homes.

Although the "squatters" who took over the farms claimed to be veterans of the war of independence in the 1970s, many of them were only in their twenties, too young to have fought in that war. Some of them admitted that local government officials paid them to take over the farms. President Mugabe donated more than $500,000 to the war veterans' group to help finance the farm invasions.

Most people agree that land redistribution is needed, but that it needs to be fair. Although the land was taken from the Shona more than 100 years ago, the farms were built by the hard work of the owners and their workers. Many Zimbabweans think these people have the right to be paid something for the value they have added to the land in making it productive.

These commercial farms account for 40 percent of the nation's export income, so losing them would be a hard blow to an already failing economy. Under redistribution, the farms would be broken into small family farms on which each family would grow its own food. This is called *subsistence farming*, and it brings no income into Zimbabwe. With the farms not producing, Zimbabwe's industries that supply them with goods and equipment laid off thousands of workers and cut the hours of others.

In addition to making statements that white Zimbabwean farmers are "enemies of the state," Mugabe sent police to bully people who were suspected of supporting the new MDC party. Its supporters were dragged from their homes by Mugabe's police force, government supporters, and other activists and were beaten or killed. Zimbabweans report being told that if they support the MDC they will die. But despite these threats, its supporters did vote, and the MDC won 47 percent of the seats in the House of Assembly in the 2000 elections.

To MDC leader Morgan Tsvangirai, this success means that Zimbabweans are tired of the rule of one man, worried about a failing economy, and concerned that corruption has broken down the operation of their government. He sees the fact that people dared to vote as an encouraging sign that Zimbabweans will meet the challenges of the future. If he is right, Zimbabwe will continue to be a shining example of how people of different races and backgrounds can work together to create a democratic African country.

In 2001, Mugabe's party continued to win the support of rural voters in parliamentary elections, while the MDC was stronger in the cities. The next presidential election will demonstrate Zimbabwe's commitment to true democracy.

Morgan Tsvangirai

Governing Zimbabwe

UNDER THE 1979 CONSTITUTION, ZIMBABWE'S LEGISLAture, the House of Assembly, elected a president to be the official head of state. The president handled many of the duties of government administration such as appointing judges and some members of the Assembly.

Opposite: **The House of Assembly**

In 1987, the Constitution was changed. Since then, one man has held the positions of president and prime minister with the title of executive president. Two vice presidents and a cabinet are appointed by the executive president. He chooses them from the members of the Assembly.

Before 1990, Zimbabwe also had a small Senate of 40 members. That was abolished, and 50 seats were added to the Assembly for a total of 150 seats. Ten of the new seats in the Assembly were reserved for traditional chiefs, 8 were reserved for the governors of each province, and 12 were appointed by the president. In 1987, a provision reserving 20 Assembly seats for whites was eliminated. Members of the Assembly are elected for five-year terms, and the executive president's term is six years.

Continuing changes to the Constitution have given the executive president, Robert Mugabe, more and more power. The balance of having a president and prime minister discuss court appointments and other issues is lost when the two positions are held by the same person.

Meet President Mugabe

Robert Mugabe was born in 1924, the son of a village carpenter. He was educated at a Roman Catholic mission school, then went to college in South Africa and taught school in Ghana. On returning to Rhodesia, he was active in forming a political party that split from the major black political party. He was arrested for subversive speech, and during ten years in jail he studied law through correspondence school.

After he was freed in 1975, he became a leader in the fight for independence from white-ruled Rhodesia. When the war ended, Mugabe's party was elected to the House of Assembly in an overwhelming vote, and he was made prime minister.

Although he planned quite openly to form a one-party government, Mugabe was careful not to alarm the whites who were the backbone of Zimbabwe's economy. For many years, he worked with them for the good of the country. The rest of the world considered him a forward-looking African leader, and Zimbabwe was known for its peaceful race relations.

In 1987, Mugabe merged his party (ZANU-PF) with the other major party (ZAPU) and soon reached his goal of a one-party state. He then combined the offices of president and prime minister to become executive president.

The Zimbabwean Flag

Zimbabwe's flag has a field of seven stripes of different colors with a white triangle at the left. In the center of the triangle is a red star with a yellow Zimbabwe bird over it. Each colored stripe has a meaning:

Green stands for Zimbabwe's plants and the resources of its land.

Yellow stands for the country's mineral wealth.

Red stands for blood shed during the struggle for freedom.

Black stands for the black majority of its peoples.

The white triangle is for peace and the path ahead. The red star is for internationalism, and it also reflects the socialist goals of the ruling political party. The bird is the famous Zimbabwe bird found at the Great Zimbabwe and other ancient sites. It represents the country's strong links with its past and its heritage.

Zimbabwe is divided into eight provinces, plus two cities that have the same status as provinces. The cities are Harare and Bulawayo. The provinces are Manicaland, Mashonaland Central, Mashonaland East, Mashonaland West, Masvingo, Matabeleland North, Matabeleland South, and Midlands. While each province has an appointed governor, the provinces do not have elected legislative bodies. They are administrative regions of the central government.

A Multiparty Republic

Officially, Zimbabwe's government is made up of representatives of different political parties, but since gaining power as both president and prime minister in 1987, Robert Mugabe has established, in practice, a single-party system, with no effective opposition to his control. This had been his intent

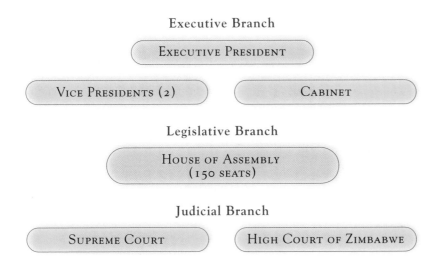

NATIONAL GOVERNMENT OF ZIMBABWE

Executive Branch

EXECUTIVE PRESIDENT

VICE PRESIDENTS (2)   CABINET

Legislative Branch

HOUSE OF ASSEMBLY
(150 SEATS)

Judicial Branch

SUPREME COURT   HIGH COURT OF ZIMBABWE

all along, as he followed a careful course, moving slowly in that direction from his first election as prime minister of the new republic in 1980. Mugabe's ruling party is the Zimbabwe African National Union, or ZANU. But groups within his own party continue to work for a multiparty system for Zimbabwe.

The most promising attempt was in 1999, when a new party, the Movement for Democratic Change (MDC), was founded. It had the strong support of the Zimbabwe Congress of Trade Unions. The backing of the labor unions gives this party more power than other opposition groups have had, and they were quickly joined by other groups including farmers, students, young people, women, and professional people who did not like the one-man rule of President Mugabe.

In the elections of June 2000, the MDC got more than 47 percent of the votes, 1 percent more than the ZANU. They won 57 of the 150 seats in the Assembly, which means that they can block any more changes to the Constitution. These amendments must have a two-thirds vote to pass.

A rally of the Movement for Democratic Change

The Supreme Court building in Harare

The Justice System

Zimbabwe's legal system is based on a combination of Dutch and English common-law systems. The president appoints judges to the Supreme Court, which has duties similar to the U.S. Supreme Court's and is the highest court of appeals. It is headed by a chief justice and has at least two other judges, but the president can appoint more members, up to a total of five.

The High Court of Zimbabwe is the other national court. It has both a chief justice and a judge president. A Judicial Service Commission of four members advises the president on the appointments, but the president appoints the members of this commission and does not have to follow their advice. So the membership of the court is almost entirely in the hands of the president.

The terms of judges are not set by the Constitution, but are decided at the time of appointment. Once a judge is appointed, his term cannot be shortened unless he resigns. Judges can be removed from office only if they are mentally or physically unable to perform their jobs, or for misconduct. If a judge is accused of misconduct, the president appoints a group of judges (or other members of the legal community who are qualified to be judges) to hear the complaints and decide.

Lower courts are made up of magistrates who decide criminal and civil cases. Separate courts decide issues of traditional African law and custom. Known as African Customary Law, these are defined in the Constitution as those laws that were in force in 1891 in the Colony of the Cape of Good Hope, which included all of southern Africa. African Customary Law includes any changes made later by Zimbabwe legislative acts. This includes the tribal law and the customs of each tribe, which are unwritten but known by tribal elders.

Outdoor meeting of a tribal court

Harare: Did You Know This?

Salisbury, as Harare was called by the Europeans who founded it in 1890, was settled at the point where the British South Africa Pioneer Column stopped its march into Mashonaland. The name *Harare*, which the city was given in 1980, commemorates Neharawe, the chief whose people had inhabited the area until it became a British colony. Salisbury was the capital of the colony of Southern Rhodesia, and it grew as a market and mining center.

Metropolitan population: 1,184,169 (1992 census)

Altitude: 4,865 feet (1,483 m)

Average temperature in July: 57°F (14°C)

Average temperature in January: 70°F (21°C)

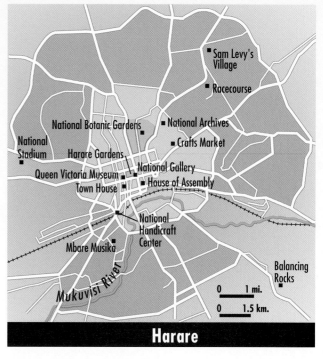

Zimbabwean law is a complex combination of several kinds of laws. These are defined in the Constitution as those rules set down in the Constitution itself, acts of the Assembly, other statutes (such as those passed by local councils), African Customary Law, and "other unwritten law in force in Zimbabwe."

The Constitution gives people the right to defend themselves if accused of a crime, and to hire a lawyer to help them. It also gives them the right to a free interpreter if they do not understand the language used in the court. While, as in the U.S. system, a person on trial cannot be forced to testify against himself or herself, in Zimbabwe refusal to testify can be considered as evidence of guilt.

Local Government

Municipal councils govern the cities together with their surrounding suburbs. Called townships under colonial rule, these outlying settlements were where blacks once lived. Whites lived in the cities, and before independence they controlled the municipal councils. Combining these areas created majority rule. Black mayors were elected for the first time in 1981.

In rural areas, where there is no municipal council, district councils have the same powers. Their members are elected by the people who live there. Candidates for these offices are

Municipal offices in Gweru

members of the same political parties that are at the national level. These local councils can impose taxes; license businesses; and provide health care, education, roads, and housing.

The Rights of Citizens

A part of the 1980 Constitution is called the Declaration of Rights, and it is somewhat like the Bill of Rights that makes up the first ten amendments to the U.S. Constitution. This declaration explains the rights of citizens. These include freedom of speech and religion, the right to own property and not have it taken away without payment, the right to move about the country, and many others.

One thing about the Declaration of Rights is quite different, however. Nearly every right makes an exception for parents to discipline their children by taking away these rights. What was unusual was that parents had this right until children reached the age of twenty-three.

In 1982, the Legal Age of Majority Act was passed, making everyone an adult at age eighteen. The act was hailed as a major step in women's rights. Before that time, all women had been considered as minors, meaning that they were controlled by their families and could not own property, get married, open a bank account, or sign a contract without permission. This act also gave women the right to vote.

Waiting to vote in the 2000 election

The Constitution also provides that any of these rights can be suspended by the Assembly during times of public emergency.

The Military

Zimbabwe's Constitution created three military branches: the Army, the Air Force, and the Republic Police. The last of these is a national police force that serves under the direction of the president.

Charges of Corruption

For many years, the government of Zimbabwe was considered to be relatively open and honest. Although minor officials did accept "gifts" in exchange for favors, and an occasional cabinet minister would seem to have a nicer home than his salary could have afforded him, the government was generally free of serious corruption. But in 1997, senior members of the ruling party, including President Mugabe's brother-in-law, were accused of claiming veteran's pensions for wounds they never received, and court evidence showed that Mugabe's wife had illegally borrowed millions of dollars from a fund. The fund was supposed to help build houses for poor people.

In 1998, the president announced that the government would pay large pensions to the president and two vice presidents, as well as to their families. Later that year, Mugabe gave himself and the fifty-five members of his cabinet 20 percent pay increases, in spite of the fact that the government was having trouble paying its foreign debt and other bills.

In 1999, the world press and many Zimbabweans questioned why Zimbabwean troops had been sent to fight a war in the Congo. They say that Mugabe spent more than $4.5 million a month of government money to obtain major financial interest in valuable mines and lumber operations in the Congo for himself and his friends.

Education

Zimbabwe has one of the best-educated populations in Africa, with a literacy rate of 85 percent for people over age fifteen. Under white rule, most of the government money spent for education went to white schools, and school was compulsory for white children ages five through fifteen. Church missions were responsible for educating black children. In 1950, there were only 12 government schools for blacks and 2,230 mission schools.

Following independence, the government made education a high priority. In the next ten years, it reached one of the highest rates of primary school attendance in Africa, with more than 90 percent of children in school. Today, education is compulsory for all children between the ages of seven and fourteen.

Schoolchildren at recess

Although the new Zimbabwean government spent more money improving public schools, the gap between public and private schools increased. Even blacks who had barely enough money to live on scrimped and saved to send their children to good private schools.

School fees were reintroduced by the government in the 1990s, which cut the number of students who could continue their education, especially in rural areas. But education is very important to Zimbabwean families, who know that it is the ticket to better jobs and future success. Families even give up necessities to pay school fees because they see education as a way out of poverty and unemployment.

Education is important to Zimbabweans.

No high school was available to blacks until 1939, and no college education until 1957. The University of Zimbabwe, established in Salisbury (now Harare) in 1955, is the primary source of higher education. Each year, 10,000 students enroll there. Other universities are located in Bulawayo and Mutare, and there are technical colleges in Harare, Bulawayo, Mutare, Kwekwe, Chinhoyi, and Gweru, as well as four agricultural schools.

Many young people go abroad for college. Most white students and black students whose families can afford it, go to Europe, South Africa, or the United States for college. Many white students also go to England or elsewhere for high school.

Because many adults in Zimbabwe grew up before schooling was available or required, the government and private agencies operate a program of adult education in the cities and villages. This program teaches people to read and write. Many educated people, including the wives of white farmers in rural areas, volunteer to teach their neighbors to read.

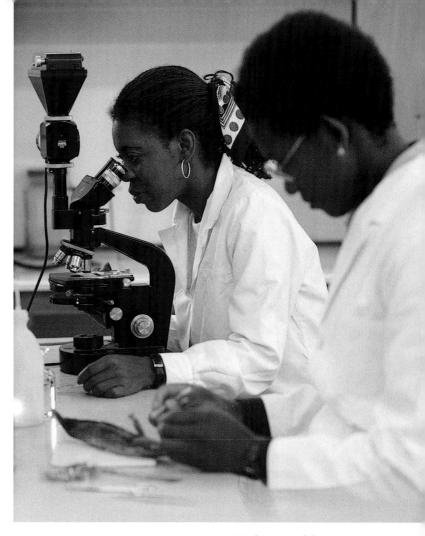

Working in a laboratory at the University of Zimbabwe

How Economics Drives the Country

S INCE INDEPENDENCE IN 1980, ZIMBABWE'S NEW GOV-
ernment has tried to rebuild the country's economy, which
was seriously damaged by international sanctions in the 1960s
and 1970s and by years of internal war. Adding to these set-
backs were the problems of poverty and unemployment.

Although at first many people wanted a socialist form of
economy and government, leaders quickly realized that this
would be nearly impossible. Systems of private ownership
were already in place from colonialism, and, despite the recent
turmoil, Zimbabwe's industry and agriculture were in good
condition and producing an income for the country.

Opposite: **A tea plantation**

A Market Economy

For these reasons, government leaders
decided that the economy would be
based on the market; in other words,
governed by supply and demand.
Today, Zimbabwe is a capitalist society. Its businesses and industries are
owned by individuals and corpora-
tions, not by the government. It is
one of the few self-sufficient African
nations, but on a personal level,
the economy is still severely in need
of help.

A landowner tilling his soil

In the early 1990s, the Economic Structural Adjustment Programme (ESAP) was organized to help solve economic difficulties. It emphasized the use of supply-and-demand tactics to motivate the economy, and to open it up to a world market. Instead of allowing the government to make every economic decision, ESAP stressed the need to let real market forces create action and economic growth.

Zimbabwe's participation in the 1999–2000 war in the Congo was expensive and created crippling shortages of fuel and other necessities. Unemployment is high, reaching 50 percent in mid-2000, and inflation is running wild at more than 60 percent per year. The people who suffer most from both these problems are the poor.

Zimbabwe's Currency

Zimbabwe's money is called the dollar. Its value has decreased steadily because of inflation. For example, in 1989 about 1.80 Zimbabwean dollars would buy 1 U.S. dollar. In mid-2001, it took almost 56 Zimbabwean dollars to buy 1 U.S. dollar.

Coins are issued as $.01, $.05, $.10, $.20, $.50, $1, and $2, and bills are $2, $5, $10, $20, $50, and $100. Coins feature wildlife or national symbols on one side and usually show the Zimbabwe bird on the other:

$2	the endangered pangolin
$1	the Great Zimbabwe
$.50	a rising sun, symbolizing independence
$.20	Birchenough Bridge over the Sabi River
$.10	a baobab tree
$.05	a hare
$.01	the flame lily

Paper money shows scenery, wildlife, or local scenes. One denomination, for instance $5, may have several designs. Among the designs on paper money are antelope, giraffes, elephants, zebras, the Great Zimbabwe, a view of Harare, rock formations, and village scenes.

The government earns about 50 percent of its income from personal and corporate income taxes. In hopes of easing the strain on the poor, the government dropped food taxes and fuel taxes. But 40 percent of its income still comes from sales taxes, which include customs duties on imported goods and taxes on hotels, taxis, communications, and other services. The remaining portion of the income comes from borrowed money and help from other countries, in the form of international aid.

Zimbabwe's major industries are agriculture, manufacturing, mining, trade, transportation, and domestic services. There is also a small trade in tourism at Victoria Falls. Agriculture and industries that supply farms employ over 50 percent of the labor force and earn 40 percent of the foreign income.

Zimbabwe's efficient farms produce a surprising amount despite the sandy soil, high erosion, and low soil fertility. In 1988, the country won a prize for "Sustainable End to Hunger," and it is nearly self-sufficient in food production. This is not typical of other countries in Africa, and Zimbabwe has been instrumental in the Southern African Development Community (SADC), which tries to help countries become more self-sufficient.

Commercial Farms

Commercial farms cover about two-fifths of the land and are generally still owned by the white minority. This continuing white ownership after three decades of independence has spurred many political problems as whites and blacks struggle

Commercial grain silos outside Harare

This farm family uses compost as fertilizer.

for power and land. But in terms of production and their contribution to the country's well-being, these large commercial farms have several advantages over the smaller, black-owned farms.

Most important, the best land is owned by the white corporate farmers. Colonial laws prohibited major land purchases by blacks, so there were few black-owned farms at the beginning of independence. Later, blacks still did not have the money to purchase this choice land from the whites.

Another major problem keeping black farmers from producing as much is Zimbabwe's poor soil. The large, productive farms can afford to buy chemical fertilizers and manure. They use this to improve land that would not ordinarily be suitable for farming. Again, for lack of money, black farmers are often unable to improve their bleak soil with expensive fertilizers.

During the first years of independence, black farmers made some progress. Programs that purchased white-owned lands and transferred them to black farmers provided

substantial resettlement through the mid-1980s. This has resulted in a significant improvement, and nearly half of the agriculture industry is now made up of black-owned farms.

Traditional housing for farm workers

The government has also tried to help underpaid and overworked farmhands by passing a minimum wage law. Although there is much debate over its effectiveness, it seems to have helped many struggling farm workers. Before the minimum wage, they were paid only a small amount, housed in shacks, and given food rations. Now the standards are a little higher. Housing and sanitation have improved in many areas, and food rations have been stopped. Workers are now paid money and are responsible for their own economic lives. Even on their low income, they can choose to spend their money to send children to school. But without food rations, they are also hit harder by inflation, which has increased the cost of food they must now buy with cash.

Inside a large tobacco auction house

Picking cotton

Tobacco is the major export crop of Zimbabwe. On a good year, the country may earn two-thirds of its agricultural export income from tobacco sales alone. This sector of the agricultural industry employs 10 percent of the workforce. Harare has the largest tobacco auction houses in the world.

The most common type of tobacco cultivated in Zimbabwe is Virginia flue-cured tobacco, although Turkish and other more specialized types are grown on smaller farms. Almost all the tobacco crops are grown on the highveld. Tobacco requires fertile soil, however, so fertilizers must be added to ensure good crops. As a result, it is often the large, well-established farms that grow this demanding but profitable crop.

Cotton, Coffee, and More

Cotton is another crop that provides export earnings for Zimbabwe. It also provides a base for the textile industry within the country, which helps Zimbabwe remain self-sufficient and keep its import costs down. Cotton's importance to the country has risen since the government urged farmers to diversify their crops in an attempt to reduce their reliance on tobacco.

Zimbabwe exports specialty coffee beans, which are considered some of the world's finest. These beans are grown mostly in the eastern highveld regions, between Vumba and

Mount Silinda. These arabica-type coffees bring a good profit due to their rarity and unique flavors.

Sugar has a double importance for Zimbabwe. It is exported as sugar, for use as a sweetener, and it is also used in the country's own fuel industry. Sugar's by-product, ethanol, enhances the usefulness of gasoline. This helps Zimbabwe to be more economically independent by reducing its need to import expensive fuels from other countries. Sugar is grown in the southern sections of the lowveld.

Livestock trade is mostly in cattle for both dairy and beef products. Beef export is a major source of income, and in

Commercial farm workers herding cattle

What Zimbabwe Grows, Makes, and Mines

Agriculture (1996)

Sugarcane	2,826,000 metric tons
Corn (maize)	2,609,000 metric tons
Wheat	280,000 metric tons

Manufacturing (1993; value in Z$)

Food products	5,329,600,000
Metals and metal products	4,107,100,000
Chemicals and petroleum products	3,153,600,000

Mining (1995; value in Z$)

Gold	2,567,100,000
Nickel	738,900,000
Asbestos	586,500,000

recent years, beef has become more popular at home. Zimbabwe has the advantage of being one of the few African countries that is approved to sell its beef to countries in the European Union. Other livestock, including goats and chickens, is raised for personal and local use. But Zimbabwe's meat production has been declining recently, and herds are smaller than at any time since independence. This is a result of the farm invasions and inflated prices.

Manufacturing

Zimbabwe's manufacturing sector is second in the region only to South Africa's. This high rate of manufacturing helps the country depend less on imports, boosting the overall economy. Foods make up nearly 25 percent of the production. Metal products, which include the refined versions of many of the country's own mining reserves, make up 17 percent of manufacturing. Textiles and chemicals make up another 30 percent of manufacturing production.

The close tie between manufacturing and other areas of economic production is one of Zimbabwe's major economic advantages. Many of Zimbabwe's raw products do not need to be exported to be turned into useful finished products. This means that Zimbabwe itself can reap more benefits from its resources. When these resources can be used within the country, it lowers the need for imports. And exported goods are worth more because they are finished, not sold as raw materials.

Natural Resources

Coal, which is found in many regions of Zimbabwe, is the country's main energy source. Coal reserves are estimated at around 30 billion tons. Hydroelectric power is also a major energy source, supplying about one-third of Zimbabwe's electricity. Electricity is used the most by industry, but more and more private and lower-income homes have electric power too.

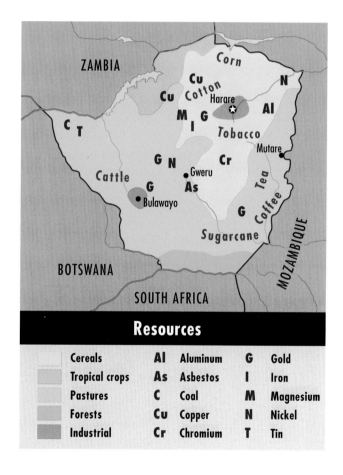

Resources			
Cereals	**Al** Aluminum	**G** Gold	
Tropical crops	**As** Asbestos	**I** Iron	
Pastures	**C** Coal	**M** Magnesium	
Forests	**Cu** Copper	**N** Nickel	
Industrial	**Cr** Chromium	**T** Tin	

An old gold mine

Nickel is an important natural resource.

Mining has always been a major player in both the economy and the history of Zimbabwe. The country has deposits of gold, silver, and platinum, which were the main attraction that brought European settlers to the area. The land also holds nickel, especially along the Great Dyke, as well as several other nonprecious metals such as iron and chrome, which are used in manufacturing. Steel, ceramics, cement, coke, and asbestos industries are all based on mineral mining.

Labor and Employment

Labor unions are active in Zimbabwe, but they were not a political force until the rise of the MDC party in 1999. They became one of the main forces behind the rise of this political party and its successes in the 2000 elections.

One of the biggest problems facing black workers trying to move up into managerial and other well-paid and professional jobs is lack of experience. Before independence, these jobs were rarely open to blacks, whose education was aimed at learning trades, not leadership skills. Blacks had little chance to gain on-the-job experience. This problem has continued into the present.

Many Zimbabweans feel that the only way for blacks to get the training they need is for companies to hire them even when they have much less experience than white people applying for the same job. This process is called *affirmative action*, or in Zimbabwe, *black advancement* or indigenization.

Most whites, and some blacks, feel that experience should be the only qualification for a job. They argue that if positions are filled by inexperienced workers, other people who have worked hard for promotions will be cheated. They also argue that employers who are paying the salaries should be free to hire the most qualified person to do the job.

One major concern is that blacks might be hired to fill high positions as a political front. In other words, blacks

A black worker gaining experience on the job

would pretend to be in charge in order to make customers and others politically happy, but the real control would remain with the white businesspeople. This began with the new affirmative action politics following independence, when Zimbabwe still had an almost entirely white-run economy. The practice diminished, but many people fear that increased pressure for black advancement will bring it back.

Should the government make laws requiring that a certain percentage of employees be black? Many people question whether such laws are wise, calling them "advancement for advancement's sake." Even many blacks feel that this process should take its natural course over time, and that trying to speed it up will only create bigger problems.

Many whites resent their loss of control of businesses they have built. They think that racism is an excuse, used to gain advantage. There are whites who encourage their black co-workers, just as there are blacks who feel that affirmative action robs them of credibility. But there are also whites who practice racism in business dealings, and blacks who take advantage of the system and of their new political power.

Black Business Ownership

Another factor that keeps blacks from having a larger share of the business economy is their inability to get loans to start businesses. To start a business, a person needs money, called *capital*. Most business owners begin by borrowing this capital. In order to get a loan, however, they need *collateral*. In other words, the person needs to own something of value that can be pledged to assure the person who is loaning the money that it will not be lost forever. The collateral is usually land or a home, and if the borrower cannot repay the loan, this property is taken instead.

Land ownership was restricted to whites during colonialism, so blacks never had the chance to acquire land or valuable collateral. Now, they have no way to start moving up the ladder. ESAP is urging the government to help people who want to start businesses to get loans. Affirmative action, in this case, would give extra help to blacks who wanted to start businesses, without interfering with the rights of other workers or business owners.

Transportation

The importance of mining since the earliest colonial days can be seen in the patterns of Zimbabwe's transportation routes. The first roads and rail lines were built to carry products from the mines, and these routes became the lines along which towns and cities grew. Today, the same routes connect these settlements.

Most of the main roads, which run across the highveld, outlining the areas most settled by the Europeans, are well kept and easy to reach. As the regions become less populated, the roads turn to dirt and to bush tracks.

Railways provide the major transportation to many parts of the country. They are especially useful in transporting manufactured goods and heavy loads such as coal. Rail lines connect Zimbabwe with its bordering countries, helping this landlocked country trade with the rest of the area. There is no significant water-transport system because the rivers are not navigable.

Trains transport heavy loads such as coal.

There is an international airport at Harare and seventeen other airports with paved runways. Bush airstrips are quite common; there are hundreds of these throughout the country. The small airport at Victoria Falls brings tourists to see the falls and to visit in the safari parks at Chobe, nearby in Botswana.

Zimbabwe's People

TWO GROUPS OF AFRICAN PEOPLES MAKE UP MOST OF Zimbabwe's 11 million citizens: the Shona and the Ndebele. The rest of the population includes white Europeans, mostly of British origin, and people of Asian descent or mixed race.

Opposite: **Ndebele woman**

Shona and Ndebele

The Shona-speaking people have lived in the great plateau that forms most of Zimbabwe since some time in the 1600s. The name *Shona* originally meant only one subgroup, but when Europeans arrived, they used the name for all the people of that language group. The Shona language is one of many in a large language group called *Bantu.* Bantu languages are spoken thoughout eastern, central, and southern Africa.

Shona man

The Matabele are a tribal division of the Ndebele. Historians disagree on the origins of the Matabele. The most common explanation, which appears in most history books, is that the Zimbabwean Ndebele were a Zulu subtribe under the Zulu leader Mzilikazi. They fled north over the Limpopo River after Mzilikazi was defeated by the powerful warrior Shaka, about 1838. They settled around Bulawayo.

**Who Lives in
Zimbabwe?**

Shona	75%
Ndebele-Matabele	18%
Other (white European, other African, and mixed race)	7%

Many modern historians disagree with this theory, however, and consider it part of a myth created in the 1850s. It was so widely accepted and taught that the Matabele themselves accepted it. But in the 1970s, scholars began to research this period and the migrations of African people more thoroughly. They now believe that the dynasty led by Mzilikazi was not Zulu, but instead came from the same general group of peoples—the Ngoni—that the early Zulus had come from. This would explain why their language and some of their traditions are similar to the Zulus'.

As you read about Zimbabwe, you will see the terms *Ndebele* and *Matabele* used interchangeably. Many people refer to the Matabele as a subtribe of the Ndebele; others use Ndebele to describe the Zimbabwean group.

In addition to these two major groups, Zimbabwe has some Tonga in the Zambezi Valley, some Venga near the Limpopo River in the south, and small settlements of Shangaan and Korekore.

**Tonga children
carrying water**

Zimbabwe is not a very ethnically conscious country, unlike neighboring South Africa, where various black groups have competed since their arrival. In Zimbabwe, the Shona and the Ndebele blend and socialize with little thought of their tribal origins. This was not always true, but their old rivalries became less important when both groups were moved off of their lands by white settlers from South Africa. After World War II, when the two began working together for African nationalism and an independent, black-governed country, these distinctions became even less important.

Shona woman

Whites are a small minority in Zimbabwe.

Other Zimbabweans

The white population in Rhodesia was not the same as in many other British colonies in Africa. They were not all from the upper classes. Most were European immigrants, usually British, who were willing to "get their hands dirty" and work hard to build a better life than they had known at home. In fact, Rhodesia actively discouraged wealthy immigrants, feeling that they were not prepared for the work that was necessary to build the colony.

So they were not a tight little group of privileged families who had known one another in England. Once in Rhodesia, they spread out on farms and missions and mining settlements. Many came from other British colonies, not from Great Britain, and although they often had been educated in England, they had not grown up there. Others were *Afrikaners*, people of Dutch origin whose ancestors had emigrated to South Africa to farm. About one-quarter of the white farmers in Zimbabwe's rural areas today are Afrikaners, also called *Boers*.

White European immigration began with the first arrivals in 1890 and became heavy after the end of World War I in 1918. By 1940, the European population numbered 70,000, and it had almost doubled by 1951, when it reached 138,000.

A small Asian community originated with traders from India and some Chinese families. Their descendants are still mostly merchants. People of mixed parentage are called *colored*. Originally, most of these were people with white or Asian fathers and black mothers, but in recent generations this group has come to include mixtures of Zimbabwe's other races as well. Some of the colored population moved there from South Africa. Socially, the colored people were somewhere between the blacks and the whites, never a part of either group.

Language

Shona was the only language spoken in the area that is now Zimbabwe until the Ndebele arrived in the early 1800s and the English settled in the later part of the same century. Today,

Common Phrases in Zimbabwe

Kanjan!	Hi!
Muri rayiti?	How are you?
Ndiri rayiti.	I'm fine.
Mangwanani; Marara-sei?	Good morning; How are you (this morning)?
Munonzani?	What's your name?
Ndinonzi...	My name is...
Tatenda.	Thank you.

English is the official language, used in schools and by the government. Only very young children are taught in their native language. Sixty-six percent of Zimbabweans speak Shona dialects and 20 percent speak Ndebele. Most Ndebele speakers live in and around Bulawayo.

Where People Live

One-fourth of the population lives in cities. Of that number, which is growing, about two-thirds live in either Harare or Bulawayo. Most of the country's working-age men live in these two cities—or at the mines where they work. Most of the women, children, and elderly people live in villages in the countryside. It is not at all unusual for men to work and live in the cities while the rest of their extended family lives in a

Many men live and work in the cities.

A woman feeding chickens

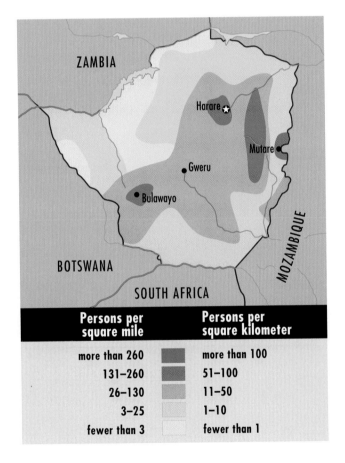

Persons per square mile		Persons per square kilometer
more than 260		more than 100
131–260		51–100
26–130		11–50
3–25		1–10
fewer than 3		fewer than 1

rural area. In the country, the family can raise crops for food, and living costs are lower. Most of the Shona live in the central and eastern part of Zimbabwe, while most Ndebele live in the west.

Few people move out of Zimbabwe to live or work elsewhere. Many whites left the country after 1965, however, and again in the late 1990s, when the government began threatening to take over white-owned farms. Children of white families, especially those who are not farm-owners, often choose to stay in Britain after finishing school there rather than return to an uncertain future in Zimbabwe.

As the economy slumped in the 1990s, more black Zimbabweans moved to neighboring countries—South Africa, Namibia, and Botswansa—to find work. But many more people have moved into Zimbabwe, however, as refugees from war and famine in neighboring countries. In the 1980s, for instance, people came from Mozambique to escape the war there and to find food and work as that country's economy fell apart.

About half the black population is under the age of fifteen, and the growth rate of the population was, until very recently, about 3 percent each year. However, AIDS (Acquired Immune Deficiency Syndrome) has struck Zimbabwe with terrifying force, and life expectancy dropped from 59 in 1989 to only 42 in the late 1990s.

Population of Major Cities

Harare	1,184,169
Bulawayo	621,000
Chitungwiza	274,000
Mutare	132,000

This grandmother cares for her grandchildren who were orphaned by AIDS.

In colonial Rhodesia, the class system was based mainly on color and economics, but also on religion and language. Afrikaners, Jews, and even lower-income whites were looked down on by upper-class English Rhodesians. Afrikaners, in turn, believed that they had a God-given right to rule over black people.

Even within the older, traditional African tribal culture, people were grouped into unequal classes. Chiefs, warriors, healers, and religious leaders formed an upper class. Under colonialism, this black elite took on jobs as police officers, tax collectors, and minor officials. In this way, they continued their role of power over other blacks. Workers were needed in the factories, farms, and households, and some of these jobs required an education, which blacks could get at mission schools. Education meant employment, and from this grew the high respect that Zimbabweans have for education. Educated people became part of the black elite, eventually producing professionals in law, education, and medicine. These people led the movement for black nationalism and independence.

Women, black or white, were not equal to men. They did not have equal education or job status, and until 1940 could not hold government jobs. Rhodesia was a world run by white British, Protestant men, but each subgroup except the poorest black rural people had another group to look down on.

Some whites questioned this society. In the 1950s, a small group of white liberals began to ask if these attitudes were still valid. But their questions were lost in the comfortable world of country clubs, household servants, and social activities. Society had become set in the ways and thinking of an earlier time—the world of explorers, missionaries, hunters, and pioneers of the 1800s. It is important to remember that the ideas of colonial times were different from those of today, and what happenned in Zimbabwe was typical of the spread of empires in Asia and South America as well.

In the first years after Zimbabwe became independent, the government changed from all white to all black. Government jobs, called *civil service positions*, were then filled by black

Government workers

workers, as were more and more professional and business jobs. New social classes grew from this. Today, Zimbabwean society is divided by economics. A new elite of wealthy blacks have joined the Europeans as the "haves," and the great majority of blacks in the lowest class are the "have-nots." There is only a very small middle class.

As blacks and whites worked together in offices, the new upper-class blacks began to have more in common with their white co-workers than with the blacks below them. Blacks had the political power and whites had the economic power. Their needs often overlapped, and they developed new working relationships. Whites and blacks still have their own friends of the same color, but even the most exclusive private club in Harare—once all-white—now has 25 percent black membership.

The relations between blacks and whites have changed with each generation. Older people tended to cling to old ideas, and the children of the first generation after independence followed their parents. But as children began sharing the same classrooms, the old barriers began to drop.

Whites, too, have different groups with different interests and goals. The two principal groups are based not on income, but on their relation to their country. One group, often called *Rhodies* (although they do not like the term) live and behave much as their colonial counterparts did. Another group, known as white Zimbabweans, are deeply committed to the country. Some of them speak Shona, and many are liberal thinkers who left Zimbabwe under the white-supremacy rule of Ian Smith and returned after independence.

Black and white school-children on a playground

Old Beliefs, New Beliefs

ZIMBABWE HAS NO OFFICIAL RELIGION, AND ITS CITIZENS are free to worship where and how they please. Before the arrival of European missionaries in the early 1890s, the Shona and the Ndebele peoples followed their traditional beliefs, which were closely tied to their everyday life.

The first missionaries to arrive represented two different Christian faiths. Jesuit priests brought Roman Catholicism in 1890, and Methodists built their first mission stations in 1892. Each provided education and medical care, along with a new religion, and the native peoples were attracted to the schools and clinics.

Adopting the new religions did not mean that the people abandoned their old beliefs. Many of them simply saw the new religion as another set of beliefs to add to their own. Others merely adopted the new religion outwardly to please the missionaries and to have access to the schools and clinics, but kept their traditional faith. Today, most black Africans follow practices of an established religion without abandoning the traditions of their ancestors.

Opposite: **A n'anga with his divining bones and sticks**

A preacher in a Tonga church

Most traditional healers are women.

The Shona revere the Great Zimbabwe as a sacred site and have done so since before Europeans arrived. Small, round houses may be used for some rituals today, but most religious gatherings take place outdoors in the villages, not in a church or other religious building.

In traditional beliefs, it is hard to draw the line between religion and medicine. The most respected spiritual figures in a village are the healers. In Zimbabwe, these people use a combination of faith and ancient herbal medicine. They give people medicines they have learned about from their elders, and many healers act as mediums, or diviners, to contact the spirit world of ancestors to advise and comfort the sick. Some of their work is similar to the laying on of hands practiced in some Christian religions.

About two-thirds of these healer-mediums are women over the age of forty. Most of them began learning these healing arts when they were younger. Not all herbal healers are also diviners.

Spirits are believed to have mediums on earth—people who can understand them and through whom they can speak to humans. Mediums usually inherit their powers, and many tell of having been taken to the spirit world for a few days when they were children and given their powers to communicate. These communications are often received when the medium is in a trancelike state.

Both the Shona and the Ndebele believe that their health and well-being depend on their spirit-guardians. These are their ancestors who have passed into the spirit world, and they protect and comfort the living. Relationships with these ancestor-spirits control people's lives, and when illness or other problems strike, they seek help from the spirits.

The mediums, who can understand the spirits, give advice based on that communication, but also based on their understanding of the patient, the village, and of human psychology. They act not only as spiritual advisors but as a combination of social worker, legal advisor, marriage counselor, confessor, and psychologist. The course of treatment they advise may be accompanied by a talisman or symbolic act, but it is often based on good judgment and a knowledge of human nature.

Roman Catholic priests near Bulawayo in the late nineteenth century

The Shona's Supreme Being is called *Mwari*. The fact that the Shona already believed in one Supreme Being made it easier for them to accept the teachings of the Christian missionaries. In addition, they believed that the spirit of an ancestor chose the oldest son as a medium in order to speak to the living. They transferred that idea to Jesus Christ, considering him to be the spirit medium of the Supreme Being. This made Christianity understandable in the framework of their traditional beliefs, not an entirely new concept.

Organized Religion

The nonblack immigrants to Rhodesia were from different faiths, mostly Christian. Of these, most were Anglican—members of the Church of England. Roman Catholics were represented by many missions, and most Afrikaners belonged to the Dutch Reform Church. Smaller Protestant faiths had missions or members. Asians were Hindus and Muslims, and there were a few Jewish congregations. Because the Roman Catholic Church supported those people who worked for independence, it was very influential in the first years of the new government.

Religions of Zimbabwe

Part Christian, part traditional beliefs	50%
Christian	25%
Traditional beliefs	24%
Muslim and other	1%

Today, these same religious groups are represented in Zimbabwe, along with some new groups that have originated in Africa and the Americas. The major one is the Zionist Church, a revivalist faith that holds large, open-air meetings with powerful sermons and dancing. This type of worship is like the old traditional village ceremonies in many ways. They, too, were held outdoors and included dancing.

Evangelical Protestant groups hold large, open-air meetings.

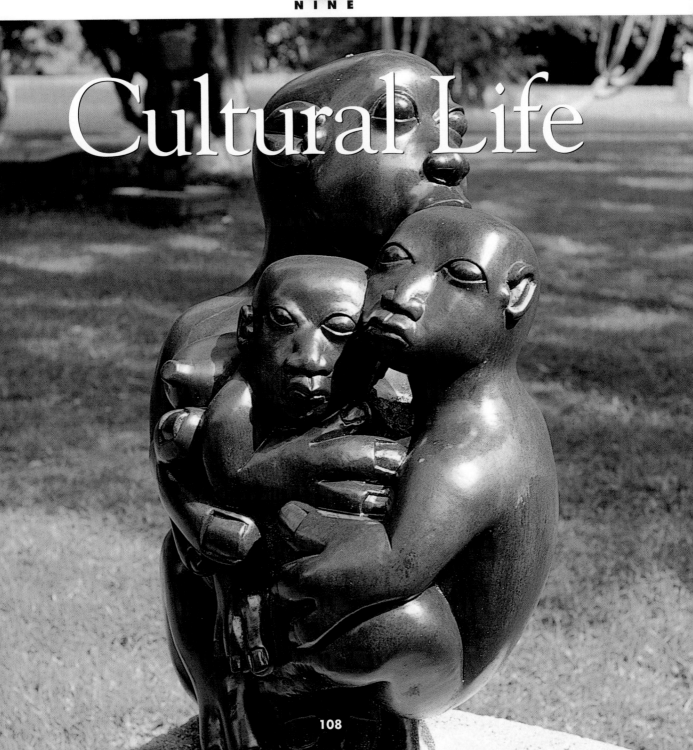

Cultural Life

B LACK AND WHITE INFLUENCES HAVE COMBINED TO CREATE a uniquely Zimbabwean culture. Music and dance are largely based on African traditions, while sports tend to be based on the influence of white Zimbabweans. Fine arts, such as painting and sculpture, are a blend of both.

Cultural traditions in the villages are largely African in origin, while city life reflects the fact that before independence only whites lived in cities. Blacks were confined to townships—totally black neighborhoods. These townships had their own social clubs. One of the interesting things about Zimbabwean culture is that it blends influences from its various population groups. This blending began even before independence.

The family is very important in terms of ancestors and protecting the family lineage. But the family is not as formalized by ritual as it is in many other societies. Marriage, for example, is traditionally more of a contract between families. The occasion may be a cause for a major celebration in the villages. Middle- and upper-class

Opposite: **A sculpture at the National Gallery of Zimbabwe**

A family poses after a wedding ceremony.

Rituals of Death

Spiritual beliefs run very deeply in both the Shona and the Ndebele cultures. Perhaps the best way to see this is in the rituals that follow the death of a family member. The Shona believe that the spirit of a dead person wanders without a home until the living family members welcome it back as a spirit ancestor.

When a person is buried, a stick is placed in the soil above the grave. After a few months, when the soil has settled into place, the stick is removed, leaving a hole in the ground. The spirit is believed to leave the grave through this hole. After about a year, the family holds a special ceremony called a *kurova guva* to welcome the wandering spirit back into the family. One member of the family is chosen as a *svikiro*, or medium, through whom the spirit is able to speak to the rest of the family. This is usually the oldest son.

The Ndebele have very similar customs. They perform a ritual called *umbiyiso* to welcome the spirit back after a year.

blacks who live in cities are more likely to have a European-style wedding celebration, as whites do. Blacks who are members of a formal church follow the traditions of that faith. But there are no formal Zimbabwean marriage traditions. Death rituals are far more important in Zimbabwe than marriage or birth rituals.

Divorce is not uncommon and was recognized by the Shona even before the arrival of the Europeans. It was less common then, simply because a divorced woman had no place to turn for support and help. But as cities grew and jobs in white households became more available, women who left their husbands had more options, although very few rights.

Women in Zimbabwe

The passage of the Legal Age of Majority Act in 1982 was a milestone in the rights of women. Under traditional Shona law, women had almost no rights at all. Marriage in Shona culture was a bond not between two people, but between two families. Male parents and grandparents made the choices. Marriage was important to the families because it created bonds that produced children in the father's kinship line.

Women had no say in this. Unlike many traditional societies, where a dowry was given to the groom's family by the bride's, in the Shona culture a bride-price was paid to the bride's family. If the husband's family could not afford the bride-price, the husband had to work for his father-in-law to pay for the wife. A typical marriage payment would have been five head of cattle, plus grain and farm tools. For families with money, a cash bride-price might replace cattle.

The new bride became the lowest member of the husband's family's household, subject to commands of her husband, his parents, his sisters, and his senior wives. She was an outsider in her new family because the ancestor spirits that protected them were not hers. She often became the scapegoat when things went wrong. Wives were often accused of witchcraft.

Women were treated as servants by husbands. Men ate alone and first, then wives ate with the children. Still, Shona women were not without some influence over their husbands. One way in which a woman had influence was in her right to name children. By naming a child "we are fallen" or "we live with adversity," she could publicly criticize and shame her husband and his family. However, women gained more power and respect as they became older and worked their way up the family order.

Although the position of women had improved somewhat before the Legal Age of Majority Act was passed, their place was still considered to be in the home, taking care of children, and tending the food garden. The missions educated women but stressed skills that would help them fill this role in the family.

Women's groups in Zimbabwe today are especially concerned with getting fair treatment under the country's inheritance laws, and with the problems that have arisen with the AIDS epidemic. AIDS has left thousands of orphans. Many of them are cared for by grandmothers or other female relatives.

Traditional Arts

Traditional arts among the Ndebele included elaborate work with beads. Tiny glass beads were first imported to southern Africa in the 1600s, and they immediately influenced the way people dressed and decorated themselves. Even before that, gold beads were brought from India. They have been found at the Great Zimbabwe and other sites, where they have been dated to as early as 1100.

Other beads were made by men, and both men and women wore beaded ornaments, but working with beads has always been a women's art. Beadwork traditions continue today, and bright beaded jewelry is sold to tourists in street markets at Victoria Falls and in the cities.

Museums About Zimbabwean Life

In the capital city of Harare are two museums that show the art and culture of the native peoples of Zimbabwe. The National Gallery of Zimbabwe has an outstanding collection that includes masks, carvings, paintings, and other art from all over the country. Behind the museum is a sculpture garden featuring stone sculptures. At the Queen Victoria Museum, displays and artifacts show how the people of Zimbabwe have lived since the earliest times.

The Shona are known for their beautifully decorated headrests, examples of which have been found at the Great Zimbabwe. These carved wooden pillows were designed to protect people's elaborate hair arrangements, which were often decorated with beads. Today, they are used by spirit mediums when they wish to communicate with ancestors.

The Shona are known for their wooden headrests.

Stone carving has developed in Zimbabwe since the creation of the National Gallery Workshop School at the art museum in Harare. This new artistic tradition began in the 1960s, when the director of the museum encouraged Shona and Ndebele artists to work in black soapstone, a soft, easily carved stone. Known as the Sculpture Movement, these artists express traditional themes from their own cultures, using materials and techniques from European art traditions.

Artists such as Sylvester Mubayi, Richard Mteki, and John Takawira have gained some notice in the international art world for their work. Takawira combines rough and polished surfaces in designs that show his own feelings about his traditional spiritual beliefs, while Metki uses highly polished stone in striking interpretations of people. Another group of sculptors, called the Tengenenge School, sculpt in serpentine, a harder stone.

Writers

An early leader in black literature was Herbert Chitepo, who was a painter as well as a poet (and a lawyer, too). Novels by Stanlake Samkange are set in the world of the Shona and the Ndebele in the time of the arrival of white colonists. His best-known work is *The Year of Uprising*, which tells about the wars of 1896–1897. Charles Mungoshi's writing looks at how

Doris Lessing

Like the people of Zimbabwe, Doris Lessing spent a good deal of her life moving about. She was born in Iran in 1919. Her father was in the British army, and in 1924 the family moved to what was then called Southern Rhodesia. In 1949, she moved to England and became an active writer. Her years in Africa colored her work, and she is well known for *The Grass is Singing* and two collections of short stories, *This Was the Old Chief's Country* and *The Sun between Their Feet*, all of which deal with her African experiences.

Shona and white cultures have clashed and mixed. He writes in both Shona and English.

A group of black writers has gained notice since independence, winning international prizes for their work. Among them are Yvonne Vera, Chenjerai Hove, and Damubzo Marechera.

Mbira Music

A traditional music style of the Shona, called *mbira*, has much in common musically with American jazz. It is based on a repeating theme through which several melodies may be woven. These melodies and the rhythm can change as a piece progresses, but always within the framework of the theme. As in jazz, there is room for improvisation but the piece is always recognizable. This makes a piece fresh and new each time it is played. Mbira is usually performed by two musicians, although one outstanding performer, Forward Kwenda, plays alone.

Playing the mbira

Many favorite Mbira pieces date back at least 500 years. The musical form itself is thought to be about 1,000 years old. At ceremonies celebrating ancestor spirits, the ancestor's favorite mbira pieces are played.

Mbira music is played on an instrument that is also called a mbira. It has long, thin metal keys mounted on a sounding board made from hardwood. It is often played inside a large dried gourd, which resonates, or echoes,

Thomas Mapfumo and Chimurenga Music

The Shona word *chimurenga* means "struggle," or "fight," and musician Thomas Mapfumo used the word to describe the protest music that grew from the fight for independence in the 1970s. Mapfumo, who was born in 1945, used his music to arouse Zimbabweans to fight for a government of their own, and to overthrow the rule of British colonials.

Ian Smith's announcement that Zimbabwe would never be ruled by Africans in his lifetime inspired Mapfumo to write a song in response. This song became popular and made him a famous political leader overnight. He was put in jail when the Smith government realized that his music was encouraging people to revolt and join the freedom fighters.

to make the sound fuller and louder. The instrument is played with both thumbs and the right index finger, which slide off the keys to make them vibrate. Each key has a different sound. Beads, shells, or even bottle caps are placed on the sounding board to create a buzzing vibration.

Perhaps it is the pleasant climate of the highveld that encourages Zimbabweans to play outdoor sports. Team sports are popular in schools and villages, especially soccer and basketball. Amateur teams gather two or three nights a week to practice on makeshift courts all over Zimbabwe. Bulawayo alone has seven teams in each of its two divisions, plus a women's team and one for boys under age sixteen. Basketball fans hope to see a national professional team soon. Rather than causing rowdy behavior at games, as sports matches often do elsewhere, basketball fans and players are very polite to each other.

Tennis, cricket, and lawn bowling are sports brought by the British. They are still played in public facilities and at private clubs.

All Zimbabweans celebrated their first sports victory as a nation just after independence, when the women's field hockey team won a gold medal at the 1980 Olympics in Moscow. Zimbabwean tennis players do well in international competitions such as the Davis Cup.

Zimbabwe's captain at bat in an international cricket match

Living in Zimbabwe

D<small>AILY</small> LIFE FOR Z<small>IMBABWEANS</small> DIFFERS GREATLY according to where they live. People who live in villages are mostly concerned with the rhythms of growing food for their families, much as their ancestors were. Women and children plant and tend gardens, while men and older boys look after livestock. Men often do the heavier work of gardening, preparing the fields by removing rocks, and digging furrows.

Opposite: **A rural village**

Men doing the heavier work of gardening

Family Meals

Along with growing much of the food, women are responsible for preparing family meals. The basic diet for most Zimbabweans is *sadza ne nyama*, usually called just *sadza*. This term is used to describe both the cooked grain that forms the basis of the meal, and the stew that is served with it. Although sadza can be any grain, it is usually made of white corn, called *mealies*. Mealies are dried and then ground in a large wooden container called a mealie pounder. Some villages have community grinding mills.

The sound of women pounding mealies is a common one in villages all over southern Africa. The pounder is usually made from a section of log hollowed almost to the bottom. It has thick sides, and is about 3 feet (1 m) tall. The dried kernels are put in the container and pounded with a long, thick piece of wood that is slightly rounded on the bottom. Once the grain has been broken up into coarse meal, it is cooked slowly until it is soft and thick, like hot cereal. Mealies are traditionally cooked in a cast iron or clay pot over an open fire.

Sadza is served with a stew made of vegetables or meat, depending on a family's

Cooking sadza over an open fire

Sadza Etiquette

When eating sadza, certain rules of behavior apply. Good manners include using the right hand to dip with and allowing younger children, who eat slowly, to get their share. Meat is not eaten at every meal, so serving sadza with meat shows that a meal is a special occasion. It is a way to honor a guest.

The size of the animal used for the meat shows the importance of the guest and the occasion. A family member who is returning after being away for several years might be welcomed with a sadza made with goat meat, while a son returning from a semester away at school might have a rooster sadza.

income. Sadza is so much a part of the Zimbabwean diet that it has become the word for any meal, too. Lunch is referred to as "sadza of the afternoon," and dinner is "sadza of the evening."

Sadza is eaten with the fingers from a central dish. After family members wash their hands, each person takes a bit of the sadza and molds it into an egg shape. This piece of sadza is dipped into the stew and eaten. The pieces of meat or vegetable are pulled out of the stew with the fingers, too.

Cities and Townships

Blacks who live in and around cities are mostly of working age. Many have families there, and some have families who live in villages. It is not unusual for a man to live and work in a city while his wife, parents, and children live in a village. But more and more young people—both married and unmarried—live and work in the cities. Help flows between city and country in both directions. The city workers can eat food grown by their family in the village, while they send money back to the family, which has few ways to earn cash.

The former townships, founded as places for black city workers to live, are still nearly all black. Life there is somewhat different from village life. Often both parents work, and many people live apart from their families.

Most whites and middle- and upper-class blacks and Asians live in the cities. Their lives are more likely to follow the European customs of the whites who established the cities. Neighborhoods are divided by economic class rather than by color—except that very few whites are poor.

Most wealthier homes in cities are surrounded by walls, gates, barbed wire, and security fences, and many have guards to protect them from rising crime. As the economy declines and more people are unemployed, this crime rate continues to grow worse.

The city home of a wealthy family

More than 25 percent of housing in Zimbabwe is considered below minimum standards. More than half a million people are homeless and waiting for the government to build promised housing, and their number is growing.

Rural Traditional Villages

Shona villages are made up of clusters of homes, usually round and built of a mixture of mud, straw, and sticks called *wattle*. Other small buildings are used to store grain, and cattle are kept in a common enclosure. A village is usually made up of several families, who may be related to one another. They farm grains, such as corn and millet, as well as rice, beans, peanuts, and sweet potatoes. Wild fruits and berries are eaten not only by the rural people who gather them, but by diners in expensive restaurants, too.

Ndebele villages are made up of groups of family homesteads called *kraals*. These may be scattered over a large area instead of grouped closely together. Traditionally, when a Ndebele man dies, his brothers inherit his wives and children, so family complexes can become quite large. The Ndebele farm corn and keep cattle for milk and as a source of wealth. Cattle are like a bank account to the Ndebele.

Newer styles of housing can be found in many villages. These include round or square homes made of brick, and homes with metal or tiled roofs. Most houses in the cities and larger towns look much like modern buildings anywhere else, although they are often quite primitive inside.

Many villages have newer styles of housing.

Leisure Time

Few Zimbabweans have their own televisions, although there are several TV stations, all controlled by the government. A network from South Africa now reaches Zimbabweans who can afford satellite dishes. Most people go to bars or other public places to watch television. Local soccer matches, dramas, and some American soaps are the most popular programs. More people—nearly 1 million—have radios, and they listen to stations broadcasting from Zimbabwe.

Amusements are mostly limited to sports, such as basketball, and gathering in local pubs. Movie theaters are rare outside of cities, but Zimbabwe is known for its popular music.

Cultural activities tend to appeal to members of all races, and the Repertory Theatre in Harare has a good mix of performers. Its plays are mostly European, not African. Drama clubs are popular in rural areas and townships. Like music, drama has become a means of political expression in Zimbabwe.

National Holidays

New Year's Day	January 1
Good Friday	March or April
Easter Sunday	March or April
Independence Day	April 18
Christmas	December 25

Although the responsibility for welfare and social services was mostly taken by missions, churches, and volunteers before independence, the government has increased its share in recent years. Not long after independence, it began a program to improve the health of all Zimbabweans. The main target was in the rural areas, where health care had been the poorest.

Treating injuries and disease was only one part of this far-reaching plan, which began with basic health issues. Education, proper nutrition and food supplies, safe drinking water, sanitary facilities, care for expectant mothers and babies, immunization against major diseases, prevention of malaria and other common diseases, and distribution of healing drugs were all part of the goal.

A mobile health clinic

Prevention was the key to much of the effort. Village health workers were trained to help each community recognize its needs and work toward immunization, good nutrition, and safe, healthy living habits. Free medical care is now available to the poor, and health insurance is provided to government and private-company workers. But even with these new efforts, many rural areas have no clinics or doctors.

AIDS has changed life in Zimbabwe. Gaining headway in the 1990s, it has struck hardest in the middle, most productive age group. Many children are now born with the virus because their parents are infected. Health authorities estimate that 35 to 40 percent of pregnant women are infected. In the age group between twenty and thirty, more than 45 percent of Zimbabweans are infected. AIDS strikes hardest at the poorest communities.

Zimbabwe is not alone. Throughout Africa south of the Sahara, more than 25 million people are thought to be infected with the HIV virus that causes AIDS. But Zimbabwe, along with its neighbors Botswana and Namibia, has the highest rate of infection in the world.

Not only has AIDS put a heavy strain on the country's already limited medical facilities, but it has strained the resources of families who must care for victims and for their children. Medical care is not easily available, with only one doctor for each 6,900 people who live in Zimbabwe. In 1996, the country had only 23,000 hospital beds, one for every 500 people. For many families, taking care of the sick and dying is a full-time job for at least one family member.

Since 1980, the government has played a greater role in health care, but disease is still serious among young children. Malaria is one of many causes of death for small children, especially in the Zambezi Valley, where malarial mosquitoes are common. Other common causes of death are measles and pneumonia, and poor childhood nutrition is a major health issue.

Timeline

Zimbabwe History

	About
Khosa peoples hunt and gather wild foods using stone tools.	500 B.C.
Khosa peoples begin making pottery.	200 B.C.
People of the plateau organize basic government systems and begin to trade.	A.D. 900
Muslims from North Africa make contact with early Shona and begin to trade goods for gold.	1000
First real communities develop; construction of Great Zimbabwe begins.	1075

	About
Mutota leaves the Great Zimbabwe to establish Mutapa.	1425–1450

Great Zimbabwe declines.	1500s
Portuguese traders arrive.	1600s
The Changamire-Rozvi gain power.	1670s
Mutapa and Changamire states remain independent.	1690–1830s
Tribal wars in South Africa cause the Ngoni to move north.	Early 1800s
Ngoni move into southern Zimbabwe.	1830s
Mzilikazi reaches what is now Zimbabwe, forging a new kingdom.	1837

World History

2500 B.C.	Egyptians build the Pyramids and Sphinx in Giza.
563 B.C.	The Buddha is born in India.
A.D. 313	The Roman emperor Constantine recognizes Christianity.
610	The Prophet Muhammad begins preaching a new religion called Islam.
1054	The Eastern (Orthodox) and Western (Roman) Churches break apart.
1066	William the Conqueror defeats the English in the Battle of Hastings.
1095	Pope Urban II proclaims the First Crusade.
1215	King John seals the Magna Carta.
1300s	The Renaissance begins in Italy.
1347	The Black Death sweeps through Europe.
1453	Ottoman Turks capture Constantinople, conquering the Byzantine Empire.
1492	Columbus arrives in North America.
1500s	The Reformation leads to the birth of Protestantism.
1776	The Declaration of Independence is signed.
1789	The French Revolution begins.
1865	The American Civil War ends.

Zimbabwe History

Mzilikazi dies; his son Lobengula becomes leader of the Ndebele.	**1868 or** 1870
Cecil Rhodes negotiates for British settlers to farm in the Ndebele lands.	1886
Rhodes gains control of all mining.	1888
Followers of Rhodes establish a small state.	1894
Ndebele and Shona rebel.	1896
Ndebele and Shona are defeated.	1897
Rhodesia becomes a British colony.	1923
Africans are forced off their farms to create bigger farms for white settlers.	1940s–1950s
Southern Rhodesia forms a federation with Northern Rhodesia.	1953
Black nationalists set up a political party, the African National Congress (ANC).	1957
ANC splits into Zimbabwe African People's Union (ZAPU) and Zimbabwe African National Union (ZANU).	1963
Ian Smith declares a Unilateral Declaration of Independence (UDI), which Britain does not recognize; the United Nations imposes trade sanctions.	1965
ZANU begins guerrilla war.	1972
The Republic of Zimbabwe is created.	1979
In the first universal elections, ZANU leader Robert Mugabe is elected prime minister.	1980
ZANU and ZAPU merge.	1987
New political parties form to challenge ZANU.	1990–1995
The Movement for Democratic Change (MDC) is founded.	1999
The MDC wins more than 47% of the vote, 1% more than ZANU.	2000
Mugabe encourages seizures of large white-owned farms.	1999–2000

World History

1914	World War I breaks out.
1917	The Bolshevik Revolution brings Communism to Russia.
1929	Worldwide economic depression begins.
1939	World War II begins, following the German invasion of Poland.
1945	World War II ends.
1957	The Vietnam War starts.
1969	Humans land on the moon.
1975	The Vietnam War ends.
1979	Soviet Union invades Afghanistan.
1983	Drought and famine in Africa.
1989	The Berlin Wall is torn down as Communism crumbles in Eastern Europe.
1991	Soviet Union breaks into separate states.
1992	Bill Clinton is elected U.S. president.
2000	George W. Bush is elected U.S. president.

Fast Facts

Official name: Republic of Zimbabwe

Capital: Harare

Official language: English

Harare

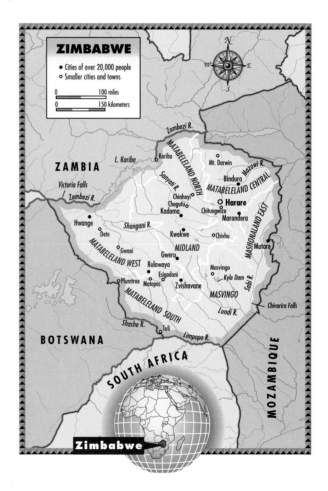

Zimbabwe's flag

Tea plantation

Official religion:	None	
Year of founding:	1980	
National anthem:	*"Ngaikom borerwe Nyika yeZimbabwe"* ("Blessed Be the Land of Zimbabwe")	
Type of government:	Multiparty republic	
Chief of state:	Executive President	
Head of government:	Executive President	
Area of country:	150,872 square miles (390,728 sq km)	
Bordering countries:	South Africa, Mozambique, Zambia, Botswana	
Highest elevation:	Mount Inyangani, 8,504 feet (2,592 m)	
Lowest elevation:	Near Dumela at the Limpopo River's exit into Mozambique, 660 feet (201 m)	
Average temperature in July:	72°F (22°C) on the plateau; 86°F (30°C) in the Zambezi Valley	
Average temperature in January:	55°F (13°C) on the plateau; 68°F (20°C) in the Zambezi Valley	
Average precipitation:	30–40 inches (76–102 cm)	
National population (1999 est.):	11,163,000	
Population of largest cities:	Harare	1,184,169
	Bulawayo	621,000
	Chitungwiza	274,000
	Mutare	132,000

Victoria Falls

Currency

Famous landmarks: ▶ *Victoria Falls,* considered one of the greatest natural wonders of Africa, where the Zambezi River drops into a gorge 300 feet (91 m) deep.

▶ *The Great Zimbabwe,* the stone ruins of a large capital that reached its height about 1400.

▶ *Lake Kariba,* created when the Zambezi River was dammed in 1959, with facilities for tourism and boating.

Industry: Agriculture including tobacco, cotton, sugar, and coffee; mining including gold, silver, and nickel; and manufacturing of food, metal products, and textiles.

Currency: Zimbabwe dollar ($) = 100 cents. In mid-2001, U.S.$1 = $55.90 Zimbabwean dollars.

System of weights and measures: Metric system

Literacy rate: 85%

Common words and phrases:

Afrikaner	A person of Dutch descent, usually one whose family came from South Africa; also called *Boer*
Boer	A person of Dutch ancestry, usually one whose family came from South Africa; also called *Afrikaner*
Chimurenga	Zimbabwean protest music of the 1960s and 1970s
Colored	People of Asian or mixed race
Kopje	Rocky hill
Kraal	Enclosure or group of buildings of one household
Mbira	Musical style and a musical instrument

Schoolchildren

Joshua Nkomo

Rhodesian	A person of non-African ancestry; usually refers to a person who supported white rule before independence
Rhodies	White citizens of Zimbabwe who do not mix with blacks and do not think of themselves as Zimbabweans
Sadza	Cooked grain served with a vegetable or meat stew; also means a meal
Veld	Open savannah and bushland of southern Africa, especially land that is farmed
White Zimbabwean	A white person who was born in Zimbabwe, considers it home, and supports democratic majority rule
Zimbabwe	Historically, the home of a chief or leader; thus, a capital

Famous People:

Doris Lessing *Author*	(1919–)
Lobengula *Chief of the Matabele*	(about 1836–1894)
Thomas Mapfumo *Musician*	(1945–)
Robert Mugabe *Executive president*	(1924–)
Mzilikazi *Founder and chief of the Ndebele-Matabele*	(about 1790–1868 or 1870)
Joshua Nkomo *Political leader*	(1917–1999)
Cecil Rhodes *Founder and leader of Rhodesia*	(1853–1902)
Ian Douglas Smith *Political leader*	(1919–)

To Find Out More

Books

▶ Beach, David. *The Shona and Their Neighbours*. Oxford, England: Blackwell, 1994.

▶ Mallows, Wilfrid. *The Mystery of the Great Zimbabwe*. London: Robert Hale, 1985.

▶ O'Toole, Thomas. *Zimbabwe in Pictures*. Minneapolis: Lerner Books, 1997.

▶ Swaney, Deanna. *Zimbabwe, Botswana and Namibia*. Victoria, Australia: Lonely Planet, 1999.

Websites

▶ **Zimbabwe Update.com**
http://www.zimbabweupdate.com
Detailed information on Zimbabwe's cities, news stories, a search engine, and more.

▶ **Mbira**
http://www.tiac.net/users/ smurungu/home.html
Dedicated to the mbira music of Zimbabwe and to other areas of its culture, food, and beliefs.

▶ **Geographic.org**
http://www.geographic.org
Statistical information on many countries, including Zimbabwe.

▶ **United Nations Cyberschoolbus**
http://www.un.org/Pubs/
CyberSchoolBus
*Information on countries of the
world, human rights issues, and
peace education, plus quizzes,
games, and much more.*

▶ **National Public Radio**
http://www.npr.org
*National Public Radio's complete
listing of news features, interviews,
and programs; you can search for
documents on Zimbabwe.*

Embassy

▶ **Embassy of the Republic
of Zimbabwe**
1608 New Hampshire Ave.
Washington, DC 20009
(202) 332-7100

Index

Page numbers in *italics* indicate illustrations.

Meet the Authors

BARBARA RADCLIFFE ROGERS and STILLMAN D. ROGERS have traveled to southern Africa several times, visiting Zimbabwe and neighboring Zambia, Botswana, and South Africa. They have written books on South Africa and Zambia for the Children of the World series, as well as a book on African safaris and another on the big cats of Africa.

Along with the books on Africa, they have written about Canada for the Enchantment of the World series. Stillman is the author of *Montreal* in the Cities of the World series, also published by Children's Press. They co-authored *Toronto* and *Vancouver* for the same series.

The Rogerses have written travel books on New England, where they live; Eastern Canada; Europe; and South America, where they have traveled frequently. Barbara and their daughter Lura, who has traveled with them since she was a child, are

co-authors of *Dominican Republic* in the Enchantment of the World Series. Both Lura and her sister, Juliette, an anthropologist, helped with the research and writing of this book.

While researching their books in Africa, the Rogerses visited the homes of local families, sharing their meals. They also interviewed rangers and researchers in wildlife parks and reserves throughout southern Africa. Although they have traveled all over the world, they remember the sight of Victoria Falls thundering into the gorge far below as one of the most memorable experiences of their travels.

Photo Credits